CLOTHESWISE

Successful dressing for your LifeStyle

E. P. DUTTON / NEW YORK

CLOTHESWISE

Successful dressing for your LifeStyle

**Alice Meyer
and Clara Pierre**

Illustrations by Charles Boone

This Book is Dedicated to

Norman Meyer

With special thanks to

Andre Pierre

George Sherry

And our editor

Marian Skedgell

———————————————————

Contents

1. A Closet Full of Clothes and Nothing to Wear

Are there too many mistakes in your closet?

- the satin evening pajamas you never wore
- the fringed Western jacket that can't go to the office
- the vested suit that makes you look anonymous rather than successful
- the caftan you bought in Mexico and haven't worn since

These are the budget-sappers, the time-wasters, the confidence-destroyers. They're taking up too much room in your closet—and your life.

"I haven't a thing to wear!" How many times have you heard

it? How many times have you *said* it? And yet your closet is stuffed with clothes. But nothing seems to go with anything else and many of the items are not appropriate for the places you go and things you do.

We all have personal clothes weaknesses. Some women can't resist a new pair of shoes but have nothing to go with them. Others keep on buying dressy clothes even though their evenings out are few. And still others acquire more lingerie than they can possibly fit in their bureau drawers, but lack enough basic clothes for every day. These mistakes are the result of hit-or-miss spending, buying without a plan—just not being clotheswise.

Why does this happen? We all do it: it's called wish-fulfillment buying. It comes from selecting clothes for the lifestyle they promise instead of letting your lifestyle determine what clothes you select.

With so many options, so many styles, shapes, colors, and textures to choose from, you often feel confused. It sometimes seems more and more difficult to put together an attractive, practical wardrobe that fills your needs.

We've all heard friends and colleagues express their doubts about clothes they've just bought. We've sensed their anxiety about what should have been a simple clothing decision and we've watched them make the same mistakes time after time.

Who hasn't been stopped by a total stranger in a department store who asks us to give our opinion about a particular dress or jacket or accessory? And who among us, before a "big" or even "small" occasion, hasn't received a telephone call asking, "What are you wearing?" Which of us hasn't wanted to ask the same question? Most women, at one time or another, have felt uncertain and frustrated when faced with putting together a wardrobe from the endless array of merchandise that's available. We can sympathize with them because we've felt that apprehension ourselves.

But there's a solution—a strategy that helps you build a compact wardrobe based on the unique requirements of the life you lead. It's called The Lifestyle Wardrobe and is based on *your* needs, *your* priorities, the way you spend *your* time. It goes where you go and does what you do. It avoids costly mistakes, saving you money as it works for you day after day. With it you'll never be faced with a time, a place, or a situation that your wardrobe can't take on.

Without it you'll never be effectively dressed no matter how much time and money you spend on your clothes.

If you have a hit-or-miss wardrobe, your symptoms are easy to spot: the thought of a department store fills you with dread; in a shop you're swayed by the salesperson's idea of what you should wear instead of holding firmly to your own. It takes you hours to dress for a simple evening out; you often refuse invitations because you're not sure you have the right clothes. You're always apologizing for the way you look; you feel threatened by well-dressed women. You never feel quite "together."

Those symptoms disappear with the Lifestyle Wardrobe. You will shop with confidence and buy only what you need. Each piece of clothing you own will go with every other and you will almost be able to get dressed blindfolded. You will always have the right thing to wear for every occasion. You'll feel secure about your looks and you'll be well on your way to the ultimate goal—a distinctly personal style.

The Lifestyle Wardrobe isn't something you buy in one afternoon's shopping spree; it's something you build slowly, one piece at a time. But once you take the plunge, your fashion confidence will grow by leaps and bounds. And one of the best things about fashion confidence is that when you've achieved it, you can't lose it. Like a good habit, it becomes a way of life.

What you'll learn as you're building your Lifestyle Wardrobe is that although you may spend more initially, your net gain will be enormous because you'll avoid costly mistakes. And taking time to think and plan at the beginning will save you money as well as many hours later on.

You'll gain a wardrobe that once set up will keep you well dressed day in, day out, without your having to think about it. In fact, the best thing about the Lifestyle Wardrobe is that once you have it you can forget about it.

Any woman can look great once in a while. The trick is to be well dressed *all the time.* Your biggest compliment won't be, "You look terrific today." It will be, "You *always* look terrific—how do you do it?"

We'll show you how.

2. The Costume Party Is Over

Remember how wonderful you felt on that special occasion when you planned your outfit from head to toe and it turned out to be not only appropriate but sensational? You were elated because you were dressed up and dressed right.

Dressing *up* doesn't have to mean dressing for a special occasion. It's just as important to look good for a meeting with your boss or your client or your child's eighth-grade teacher or while you're marketing, exercising, or making dinner. When you're dressed "up" you feel "up." Whether your goals are personal or professional, or a combination of the two, the "up" feeling helps to get you there. It's a feeling you can have every day but it doesn't come by accident.

4

It has to be thought out, mapped out, planned. That's being clothes-wise.

First you must know who you are. Clothes can't give you an identity. Instead, your clothes should take on their character from *you* and your life. Today's clothes are a tool, a way to make a statement about yourself, your aims, and aspirations.

It hasn't always been so: Women have allowed themselves to be dressed as Russian peasants, cowgirls, *Star-Trek* zombies, jocks and gymnasts, chairpersons of the board, punk motorcycle molls, and college "preppies." But such disguises are irrelevant to real life. A motorcycle jacket doesn't inspire confidence at an office meeting and a Peruvian poncho isn't the best thing to wear for a job interview.

The costume party is over. It's time to learn how to dress for the life you lead. You and you alone. And planning ahead is more necessary than ever, because today you're up against a whole new set of circumstances:

Clothing prices have escalated to the stratosphere. Cost alone makes trying on "identities" by means of clothes out of the question. Today you need clothes that give you the *most* for your money—clothes that move from day to day, day to evening, season to season. It's extravagant to wear a suit only one way. It's uneconomical to feel you must have a wardrobe of evening wear. It's dated thinking to buy fabrics that work for only one season.

RISING COSTS

LESS TIME TO SHOP

We don't have to tell you why. The woman with a multifaceted life needs a wardrobe that will see her through her various roles efficiently, without wasting her time on unnecessary decisions and dilemmas about what goes with what.

A BEWILDERING CHOICE
OF MERCHANDISE

Style changes are more rapid and confusing than ever, while simultaneously the choice of what to buy grows larger and more overwhelming.

NO FASHION DIRECTIVES

To make matters worse, there's no one way to look anymore. Not that there isn't fashion news—there's almost too much of it. But the biggest fashion news isn't where we're accustomed to finding it—in the designers' collections. The designers themselves are no longer dictating "this season's silhouette" . . . "that season's color."

The new freedom in fashion can make shopping a rewarding adventure, but freedom always exacts a price. The other side of the coin is that without any of the old rules to guide us, we can find ourselves at a loss when it comes to fashion choices. And ironically, while there is less direction coming from the fashion world, clothes themselves have more power than ever. They are a tool we can't afford to ignore. Even a woman who knows very well who she is and where she's going needs *more* help now in charting her way through the fashion confusion. She needs a whole new strategy for a new set of circumstances.

What is it that has made fashion a tool instead of a goal? It's partly that women themselves are more ambitious, more active. They lead multifaceted lives, lives filled to the brim with career, home, husband, children, friends, sports, community involvement, active interests of all sorts. Put it down to the women's movement, chalk it up to the statistics: More than half of American women work, and the numbers continue to climb. But whatever the cause, what we've got is a real transformation in how women live their lives. And consequently, there is a mammoth change in the demands they put upon their wardrobes.

You need to choose clothes that give you some leeway: not the floral dress that requires you to buy a special bag and shoes for it alone, but a solid-color, two-piece silk whose parts can be worn with other items you already own. You want versatility: a braid-trimmed jacket that looks as right at cocktails as it does at the office. And you want performance: silk pants that team with a silk blouse or tunic when it's warm and a fuzzy sweater when it's cold.

What this all means is a change in the way you plan, shop, and organize your closet. What it adds up to is an entirely new formula for dressing: a wardrobe that exactly corresponds to the life you really lead.

The secret? Learn to identify the clothes you need to play the most important role of all—yourself.

3. Taking a Lifestyle Inventory

Most of us face it every morning: the hurried look at the clock, the mad dash to the closet, the chaos behind the closet door, the dreadful question, "What shall I wear?" the feeling of helplessness, the halfhearted attempt to put together an outfit that will work for the crowded day ahead, the doubt that your choice is right, and, finally, the inevitable reach for an old standby.

Perhaps you, like most women, wear ten percent of your clothes ninety percent of the time. Ever wonder why? Because those are the clothes that fit the way you really live—that meet your actual needs. They're the solid core of your wardrobe that can be worn over and over. The clothes you reach into your closet for time after time are those based on the day-to-day reality of your life.

What of the other ninety percent? They're the clothes that are invariably never worn because they don't fit, are unflattering, or are inappropriate for the places you go and the things you do. For example:

- the styles you left behind—the sorority sweater, the rock-concert jeans, the flea-market jacket, the three-piece beige "success suit," the glitzy disco dress, your going-away ensemble

- designer's fashion fantasies—the Mini, the Micro, the Midi, the Maxi, Mod, Punk, Retro, and Peasant

- "mistakes"—those items you bought on impulse or on an off-day or for a one-time occasion

If any of these items gives you a little shock of recognition, now is the time to think hard about your life. Then think about your clothes. Are the two synchronized? Or do you have a jet-set wardrobe for a work-a-day life? Do you collect active sportswear and never move a muscle? Do you buy party clothes and stay at home? Do you fall for glamorous loungewear and live in jeans? Are you allowing the fashion designers to sell you a lifestyle you don't own? No wonder you don't have anything to wear!

You *are* capable of putting your wardrobe in order, even though every woman's clothing needs today are far more complicated than they were just ten short years ago. But, until now, no one has come up with a system of wardrobe management. You've been shown how to organize your time, your career, your home, and your finances. Who has taught you how to put your clothes-life in order?

That's what the Lifestyle Wardrobe is all about.

It can't be said too often: Your needs should determine your clothes. The first step is to fill out your Lifestyle Chart, which is the key to synchronizing your clothes and your life. With the chart as a guide you put an end to chaos and take control. The chart puts you in charge of your clothes-life. It gives you the tools to end the confusion that exists behind those closet doors. It makes your clothing dollars work for you instead of against you.

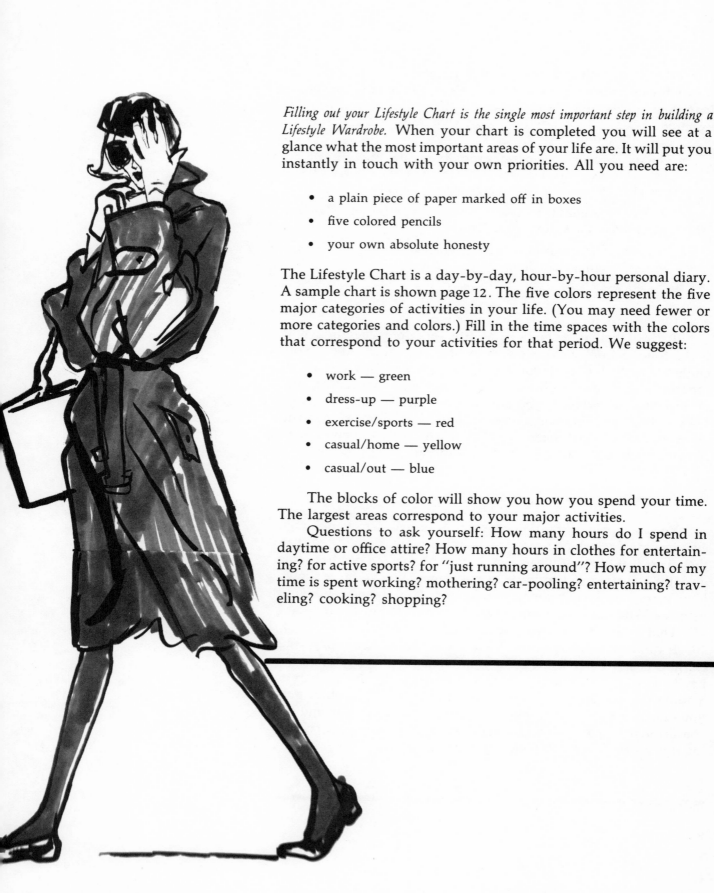

Filling out your Lifestyle Chart is the single most important step in building a Lifestyle Wardrobe. When your chart is completed you will see at a glance what the most important areas of your life are. It will put you instantly in touch with your own priorities. All you need are:

- a plain piece of paper marked off in boxes
- five colored pencils
- your own absolute honesty

The Lifestyle Chart is a day-by-day, hour-by-hour personal diary. A sample chart is shown page 12. The five colors represent the five major categories of activities in your life. (You may need fewer or more categories and colors.) Fill in the time spaces with the colors that correspond to your activities for that period. We suggest:

- work — green
- dress-up — purple
- exercise/sports — red
- casual/home — yellow
- casual/out — blue

The blocks of color will show you how you spend your time. The largest areas correspond to your major activities.

Questions to ask yourself: How many hours do I spend in daytime or office attire? How many hours in clothes for entertaining? for active sports? for "just running around"? How much of my time is spent working? mothering? car-pooling? entertaining? traveling? cooking? shopping?

For example, if you're a single businesswoman living in a big city, your work probably takes up most of your time. The largest block of color on your chart will be green and your primary need is for clothes to help further your career goals. If you spend most of your leisure hours at home whipping up casual dinners for your friends or just curling up with a book, the yellow area on your chart may be almost as big as the green. Your second most important need is for casual clothes for those at-home hours. You dress up just one night a week? If so, the purple area on your chart will be the smallest. Your need for dressy clothes is slight.

Or you've taken a leave from work to raise two small children. Not used to being housebound, you've made sure you put in two mornings a week at the gym. Your need to be "out in the world" is satisfied by working as a hospital volunteer once a week. Your social life centers around weekend evenings at the country club.

LIFESTYLE WARDROBE CHART

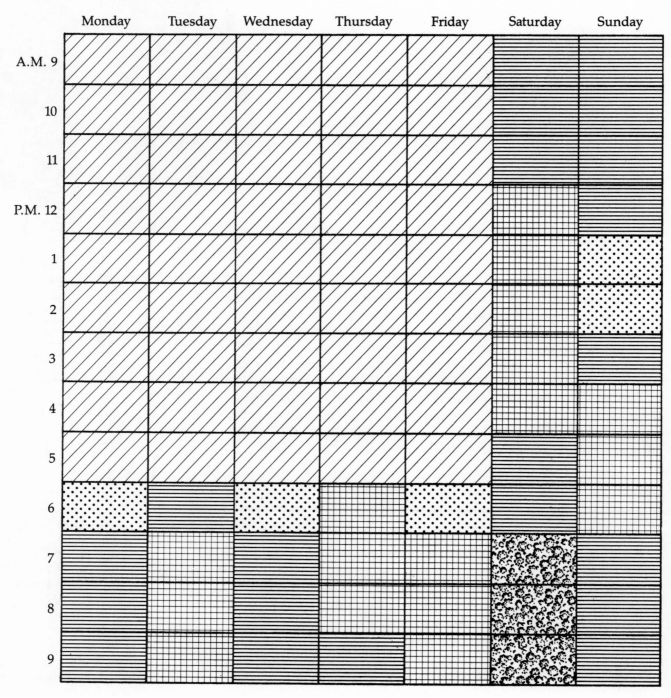

Work (*green*)

Dress-up (*purple*)

Exercise/Active Sports (*red*)

Casual Home (*yellow*)

Casual Out (*blue*)

	Monday	Tuesday	Wednesday	Thursday	Friday	Saturday	Sunday
A.M. 9							
10							
11							
P.M. 12							
1							
2							
3							
4							
5							
6							
7							
8							
9							

Multifaceted is a word that seems to have been coined just for you. Your chart will show it: Red to start out those two days of exercise, green for the hospital afternoons, purple for your evenings out. But your largest block will undoubtedly be blue and yellow, for your life is basically being at home or out-of-doors with the children and doing errands for the house.

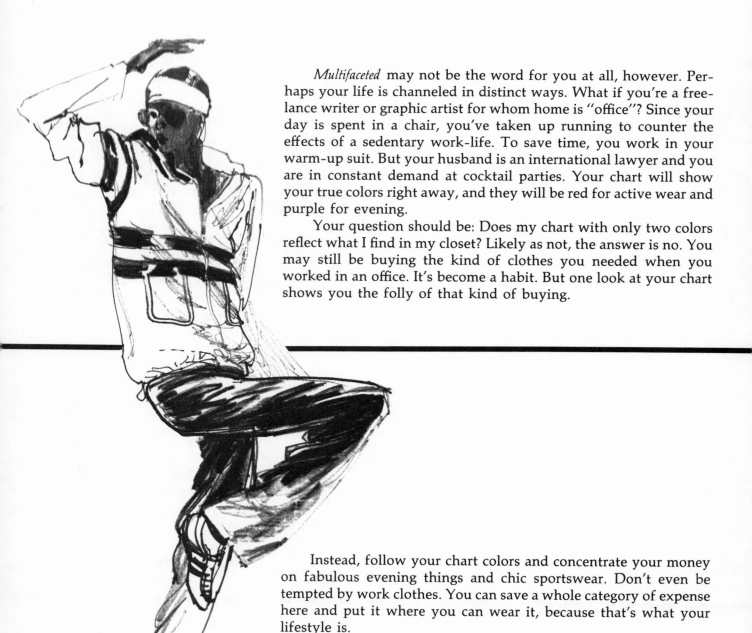

Multifaceted may not be the word for you at all, however. Perhaps your life is channeled in distinct ways. What if you're a freelance writer or graphic artist for whom home is "office"? Since your day is spent in a chair, you've taken up running to counter the effects of a sedentary work-life. To save time, you work in your warm-up suit. But your husband is an international lawyer and you are in constant demand at cocktail parties. Your chart will show your true colors right away, and they will be red for active wear and purple for evening.

Your question should be: Does my chart with only two colors reflect what I find in my closet? Likely as not, the answer is no. You may still be buying the kind of clothes you needed when you worked in an office. It's become a habit. But one look at your chart shows you the folly of that kind of buying.

Instead, follow your chart colors and concentrate your money on fabulous evening things and chic sportswear. Don't even be tempted by work clothes. You can save a whole category of expense here and put it where you can wear it, because that's what your lifestyle is.

Whoever you are, however many or few your colors, your Lifestyle Chart will show you what your clothes-life should look like. You've filled out the chart: It's instant recognition, the first step. Now you can use this knowledge to synchronize your clothes priorities with your life priorities.

The key question to ask yourself is this: Is the largest category on my chart also the one for which I own the most clothes? Say, for example, that you blocked out most of your spaces in green. The same proportion of work clothes should show up in your closet. That's the Lifestyle Wardrobe principle in operation.

As a bonus, your Lifestyle Chart is useful in budgeting your clothing dollars. The biggest block of color deserves the largest percentage of your budget. Conversely, the smallest deserves the least. For example, for most women evening clothes are a relatively small category. Because they're exciting—and expensive—the temptation is to overbuy. That can wreak havoc on your clothes budget. Put your money where you put in the most time. Later in this book we'll give you strategies for getting around expensive one-time purchases and other budget breakers.

Once you've filled out your Lifestyle Chart, the next step is to learn how to avoid the fashion myths that have contributed to that pile-up of clothes you rarely wear.

4. Forgetting the Fashion Myths

You already know the fashion "rules": tall women should wear low heels and short women should wear monochromatic colors and scaled-down accessories. These are old-fashioned camouflage techniques, based on the notion that clothes can work optical illusions—if not miracles—on basic body structure. Instead, those dos and don'ts just take all the pleasure out of clothes and inhibit your personal style.

It's time to recognize the rules for what they are: Fashion Myths. It's time to tear them up and replace them with new options. For example: A short woman *can* wear bright-colored shoes and hose. If she adds color at the neckline and keeps everything in between a solid shade, she'll look taller instead of shorter because color at the extremities draws the eye outward. Tricks like this just go to prove that you can shape fashion to *your* figure.

The point is not to get hung up on your figure "flaws." We've all seen those magazine articles that feature charts showing how to make yourself look taller, slimmer, less hippy, less bosomy, or whatever fits the current ideal by camouflaging your imperfections with monochromatic colors, horizontal stripes, and V-neck blouses. But where do these rules lead you? If you're short you'll just look like a short woman wearing a single color; if you're tall you'll stand out even more in horizontal stripes; and a V neckline can't possibly disguise an ample bosom.

Those antiquated charts are based on the notion of ideal proportions. If there were only *one* idea of physical perfection would we consider both Audrey Hepburn and Sophia Loren beautiful?

So the first Fashion Myth to throw out is camouflage. Too often it backfires, calling attention to what we most want to hide. A scarf can draw the eye straight to a less-than-perfect neck. A long skirt, when short lengths are in vogue, focuses attention on heavy calves. Wafer-thin heels only serve to unbalance and emphasize their wearer's height. In other words, "correctives" show. It's better to accept your body type and work from there. *Clothes can enhance your figure but they can't change it.*

What this means is that your shape doesn't have to meet certain requirements in order to look well in a particular style. The idea of the body dictating how you should dress is outmoded. Short or tall, thin or heavy, you can learn how to shape fashion to *your* size. And any fashion rule that interferes with this is going to have to go. For any look is possible if you know how to make it work for you.

Take the jacket on these pages. It's an avant-garde version of a classic blazer, designed for an average figure. A big woman might consider the broadened shoulders and loose line too exaggerated; a small woman might shy away from a jacket like this, thinking it too large-scaled for a petite—*if* they're going by the old rules. But look again. On the 5 foot 10 inch woman the jacket is casual, easy. Put it on a woman 5 feet 2 inches tall and you have a very neat look, not at all overwhelming. How to adapt it to either body type? It's a learned skill that means paying attention to details.

Proportion depends on context: The tall woman is wearing the jacket belted, with her sleeves rolled up (or cuffs turned back) and a large shawl thrown casually over one shoulder. The short woman wears her lapels turned up and adds a small beret to create a taller look. The unbuttoned jacket reveals a slim, self-color belt at the waist.

Once you've banished the idea that clothing should be used to camouflage the body, you're ready to extend your new approach to the clothes themselves.

Are you taking certain fashion rules for granted? What used to be hard-and-fast rules are really old-fashioned myths. Let's explode some of these myths:

**MYTH:
DON'T BE SEEN
IN THE SAME OUTFIT
TOO OFTEN**

Do you avoid wearing the same outfit for the same "audience"? Does it bother you to wear the same clothes two days in a row? It shouldn't. Do you ask yourself, "Have I worn this dress to the Smiths' before?" It doesn't matter if you have. The new attitude says: I'm assured enough to wear the same dress twice. Not: I have to have a new outfit for each occasion. That's old-style insecurity.

**MYTH:
AGE SHOULD
DETERMINE DRESS**

Remember we said that you can wear anything, if you learn how to adapt it to your own style? That goes for age, too. Today women are looking differently at the question of aging. And what emerges loud and clear is: options. In the past, when a woman of forty was considered over the hill, it seemed fitting for her to dress modestly, even somberly. Nowadays, a woman of seventy can be actively involved, running a business, heading an organization. You can bet that she doesn't want anything to do with "old-lady dressing."

The modest jacket dress has gone the way of widow's weeds. Just as there are no age limits to being active, there are no barriers to dressing for an active life at any age.

FIVE UNIFORMS

A working woman we know puts together five uniforms—one for each working day—at the beginning of each season. Some are remakes from her closet, some are new. Her efforts go into alterations and accessories so that every day she wears a perfect working outfit, even though it's been seen the week before.

20

A DOZEN DRESSES

A corporate wife confided that her closet contains twelve sensational silk dresses, bought over a period of time. Seasonless, they can be worn over and over again. "I never grow tired of them. My friends don't either. In fact, they've begun to borrow my clothes strategy."

Don't do it: clothes don't age like wine. Even classics get modified, as you'll see later on. Your body can change. Your color preferences can be fickle.

Our Puritanical tendency is to save new purchases for "good." But this way, their hardest wear comes at the end of their life cycle instead of at the beginning. Their effectiveness should be up front, where it's bound to have the most impact, and to give you the most pleasure. Why miss the chance to feel good in a new purchase right away? In this case saving can be wasting. And you'll be seen *most often* in clothes that are two or three years old. Reverse the procedure.

MYTH:
SAVE NEW CLOTHES FOR
SPECIAL OCCASIONS

Give those linen separates a second life. Try them under a sweater-vest. Pop a velvet jacket over both. Cotton-string knits, silks, rough woven blends, velours, silky synthetics, and most ethnic clothes are truly season-spanners.

Color is no longer confined to a particular season. Black makes a perfect summer look—there's nothing like it to show off a tan. Winter-white can give you the most elegant cold-weather look of all. Patent leather and canvas accessories used to be relegated to summer; now they're in action all year round.

MYTH:
SUMMER CLOTHES
CAN'T BE
WORN IN THE WINTER

MYTH: NEUTRALS ARE BLACK, BROWN, AND NAVY

√

Nonsense. Black doesn't go with the brown family; most browns don't work with black, and navy looks best only with itself, red, and white. Nothing has changed more dramatically than our sense of color and its possibilities. Today we have a new set of neutrals. They're aubergine and acid green. They're curry, copper, mauve. No, you're *not* taking a big chance by buying a bright red blouse. It will see a lot of use with colors on both sides of the spectrum: the warm and the cool tones.

The definition of a neutral is that it goes with almost anything. Take red a step further. It does more for other colors than any of the old-style neutrals: it's a color catalyst. No matter what your colors are, red will rev them up. If your wardrobe is composed of classic, cool monotones—that range of beige-gray-navy—red is what you need to heat things up. How about red with offshades and pastels? Think of it with khaki. Picture it with the pales: yellow, blue, pink. It works. See it with salmon, mauve, all the earth shades of sand, rose, mustard, olive; the sophisticated offtones of greige and taupe.

What about those aubergines and acid greens? The coppers and mauves? Use them just as you would red or any of the old-style neutrals: to bind color families, to give life to monotones. Our eyes have become accustomed to a whole new range of color combinations—pink and orange, teal and purple, silver and bronze, olive drab and cinnamon. With a palette like that, no wonder neutrals aren't neutral anymore.

The fact is that any color goes with any other. Think of a color wheel: the colors composing it flow, they're harmonious. Any one of them can act as a catalyst—a "neutral"—for any other. Where you come in is in regulating tone, intensity. Playing with color possibilities, assigning an unexpected color a "neutral" function, is one of the surest ways to sophisticate your total look.

MYTH: ACCESSORIES SHOULD BE NEUTRAL

√

The place to start using the new neutrals is in accessories. One of the best rules to break is: "White shoes are for summer." Wear them with your winter whites instead. Patent leather is no longer relegated to summer either. Black patent leather gives a wonderfully finished look all year round, especially with tweeds, plaids, and gray flannel. The most dated rule of all, "Handbags and shoes must match," now has options. Your shoes and bag can match; they can be in the same color family; you can choose a multicolor handbag in which your shoe color appears. In fact, a bag patterned with many colors is one of the best new accessories you can buy. It gives you a whole range of colors to work with, to highlight your whole ensemble or to echo another accessory. And it gives you a terrific way to break another one of those old rules: Don't mix patterns.

F ashion designers make a point of mixing patterns—look at some of YSL's best styles. Different prints or patterns do mix harmoniously—provided they have a similar feeling and scale, and the colors are in the same family. Plaids, prints, and stripes can be successfully combined if the patterns are subtle and in the same tones. A small-scale floral print could mix with a same-scale stripe or geometric, and with similar fabrics and colors you could even mix two stripes.

MYTH:
NEVER MIX PRINTS
OR PATTERNS

W hen an invitation specifies black tie, your escort knows exactly what to wear—a dinner jacket. But for you, there are options. Even the most formal occasions don't necessarily require a long dress. A short cocktail dress with glittery jewelry, high heels, and shimmery hose would make you look just as dressed up as a long dance dress. Elegant silk pants with a dressy blouse or camisole, or a beaded sweater, can work just as well. And evening pajamas may give you the most dramatic look of all.

MYTH:
WHEN THE INVITATION
SAYS "BLACK TIE"
YOU MUST WEAR A
LONG DRESS

**MYTH:
LOUNGEWEAR IS JUST
FOR LOUNGING**

If you obey this rule, you're missing out on a lot of fashion extras:

- the Chinese kimono that makes a perfect lightweight evening wrap
- gold mules that go out to dinner with harem pants or evening pajamas
- a caftan, boldly belted, that takes a night off from hostessing and goes to someone else's party.
- even that slipper-silk nightgown—see if the evening-wear collections aren't selling the same idea at twice the price!—But before you wear it out check it in a good strong light to find out if it reveals too much.

**MYTH:
SPORTSWEAR IS FOR
ACTIVE SPORTS**

By reshaping your thinking you can extend your wardrobe. Consider, for example, the following possibilities for evening wear:

- The cotton camisole you play tennis in can lead an evening life. Seeing it with silk pants and an interesting necklace, no one would know how it spent the day.
- Leotards give you a dazzling array of tops for bare evening dressing. A long taffeta skirt and an attention-getting sash make good partners.
- The pants of a velours running suit can be a witty accompaniment for a silk blouse. Accentuate the counterpoint by wearing the blouse open at the neck and sporting a spill of gold chains.

Remember, the easiest sportswear to transform to nighttime dress is apt to be black or white. These look more dressy to begin with.

Business and professional women have been told they need no-nonsense, businesslike clothes much like their male colleagues wear in order to succeed; that to get ahead in what has traditionally been a man's world, we have to dress like feminine equivalents of men. But *you can succeed in business without a suit!* And you can do it in clothes that are attractive and womanly.

The standard "success uniform" is a two- or three-piece suit (always with a skirt) in navy, gray, or beige; a silk blouse in an unobtrusive color (off-white with an ascot or bow neck is the number-one choice here); basic pumps and sheer, neutral hose. These will, we're told, put us on a fast track to the executive suite. But is it necessary to dress this way to make it in business? We say no.

The truth is that clothes alone won't get you ahead. If you're not competent all the three-piece suits in the world won't help. And there's nothing wrong with being competent and fashionable. Being both can give you an edge: a keen fashion sense will underline your competence.

Of course the uniform is safe. It's also boring. And, on many women, unattractive. Even though some professions are more conservative than others, that shouldn't condemn you to looking dowdy and dull. Most likely your male colleagues aren't going to forget you're a woman no matter how nondescript you try to look —so why should you? You can look pretty and still look professional. You don't have to leave fashion at home when you go to the office—it's as welcome in the business world as it is anywhere else.

You don't have to follow suit to get ahead. Imagine this scene: a meeting at the corporate headquarters of a large insurance company. Three women, all heads of their respective departments, enter the conference room. The first wears a print dress with full sleeves and a matching ruffle-edged scarf at the neck, sling-back pumps, and she carries a handbag and attaché case. "When I first came to the company I suppose I was intimidated by my new responsibilities," she admits privately. "I hid behind the standard three-piece suit. But looking like one of the boys wasn't for me. I adore dresses. I guess I don't mind people seeing that I have good legs. Gradually I began to feel enough confidence in my performance at work to go back to them, and I haven't stopped wearing dresses since. They're my trademark, as a flower or a scarf is for another woman."

The second woman is a self-proclaimed fashion hound. Adores color. Lives in imports when she can splurge on them. Today she sports the latest outfit from her favorite designer: pinstripe trousers with an oversize sweater set woven in a giant Argyle pattern. On her wrist is a wide polished silver cuff. She carries both personal effects and business papers in a large kidskin shoulder pouch. Her clothes authority is unquestionable, and she brings the same confidence to her job. She likes the feeling of ease that good clothes give her. "I find suits restricting," she says, "and I hate being uncomfortable. I think that you should be *noticed* at work. Women especially don't get promoted by disappearing into the woodwork."

The third woman wears her "power suit." She never carries a handbag, always an attaché case. She claims her "uniform" got her where she is today, but everyone else knows she just has a talent for business. She has five of these suits and they work well for her for a good reason: she doesn't like spending a lot of time putting herself together. Once she knows she's appropriately dressed and comfortable in her clothes, she can devote herself to other things.

These three women, completely different in their fashion philosophies, would agree on one point—dressing for business is a matter of options, not rules.

**MYTH:
THE LATEST DESIGNS
MAKE YOU LOOK
FASHIONABLE**

Don't confuse style with fashion. Fashion is of-the-moment and doesn't always confer style upon the wearer. And clothes that are in fashion one year are often out the next. Your wardrobe should include some clothes that are *not* in fashion. These should be pieces that are distinctive enough to be independent of—outside of—current fashion and so well suited to you and your lifestyle that they'll go on making you look stylish year after year.

**MYTH:
TAME, NONCOMMITTAL
CLOTHES GIVE YOU THE
MOST WEAR**

Colorless clothes seem to offer the promise of repeated wearings, but by being anonymous they're also without style. The tried and the true can become dull and ineffectual, and a wardrobe built entirely of familiar classics becomes tiring. Be sparing of good, sensible clothes. You may *keep* them for years but *wear* them less often than you think. Extreme styles may give you just as much—or more—wear than basic styles. True, you may tire of them sooner, but during their shorter life-span they may give you more pleasure—and more wear. And when it comes to clothes, longevity is less important than wearability.

**MYTH:
CLASSICS ARE ALWAYS
TRADITIONAL**

What is a classic? Is it a camel polo coat or a Moroccan caftan? Is it a velvet blazer or a Chinese brocade jacket? Today it's all of these. Real classics are serviceable, familiar, adaptable. But they're *never* boring.

What's new about classics now has a lot to do with things other than fashion. Changes occur so fast in our lives that a "look" can get trashed almost before it's worn. The speed at which things happen can grate on us all. One alternative is to go back to safe clothes—the dumb classics left over from our school days. A better way is to cull what's worked best from decades past. But we don't mean "nostalgia." What we have in mind are the all-time greats, mixed with those items of antique or ethnic cast which American women are good at tracking down in flea markets and attics or in bazaars and shops around the world.

For there's another new fact in our stepped-up lives: travel. Who can resist the temptations of an Irish fisherman's sweater or a Mexican poncho? Or, for that matter, our very own Texas cowboy boots or down parkas? These classics are universally wearable. We call them Eclectic Classics. And we don't leave out the possibility of their being downright eccentric. But being eccentric doesn't keep something from being worn again and again.

In fact, one of the best things about fashion today is that you can take your pick. Living in a time of fashion freedom has its advantages. There's no one around to tell you how you must look from one moment to the next. It's natural to return, time and again, to styles that are durable. Even avant-garde designers are looking into closets and pulling out old-but-terrific ideas. Like sweater sets and embroidered ethnic jackets. Why not cull what's good from the past, and stick with it? We all have at least one Eclectic Classic, and sometimes several.

Seventh Avenue knows an Eclectic Classic when it sees one. Look at the tweed blazers coming off the line: they're based on the riding jacket that has had the same design for hundreds of years. Look at the "Chanel" suit that has resurfaced in this country. The streets are filled with women wearing kilts, Fair Isle sweaters, prairie skirts and cowboy boots, for casual wear.

We think Eclectic Classics are going to be the clothes of the 1980s because, quite simply, they reflect the way we live. And if you haven't cultivated them over the years, the proof that they're classics is right there in the stores. They're always available. Some may disappear for a season or two, but they all resurface sooner or later.

Here's our list of Eclectic Classics. It's basically a summary of ideas, not a shopping list. You'll have some of your own favorites to add:

- lace-trimmed Victorian blouses
- embroidered velvet jackets
- kimonos, caftans
- kilts
- cowboy boots
- "le smoking" evening suits
- riding jackets and jodphurs
- fisherman's bags
- loden jackets
- peasant skirts and shawls

Now that you've laid to rest the Fashion Myths and taken a fresh look at your Eclectic Classics, you can dress creatively—and get new looks from old—by finding different ways of wearing what you already own.

Remember the 1960s, when it was all the rage to wear an extravagant silk shirt with jeans? That was the fashion equivalent of driving up to McDonald's in a Mercedes-Benz. Juxtaposition: It gives your look shock value. What's fashion for if not to keep your audience wide awake and noticing you?

So shake up your wardrobe by mixing the "un-mixables." A leather or suede jacket looks especially appealing over a lacy Victorian blouse. A man-tailored tweed blazer becomes soft and elegant when worn with a lace-trimmed silk blouse. A cotton shirt alters the strict mood of a cable-knit shetland sweater if you add a lace collar and a low-slung cord belt. Versatile clothes lend themselves to mixing: A dressy blouse can look as good with a pair of jeans as with velvet pants or a silk skirt. A mix of moods adds extra excitement.

Another way of surprising the eye is to wear intense colors together. It's not true that two or more brights will clash. Travel has made our color sense more sophisticated. Thanks to the color ideas from Mexico, we've discovered that hot pink and orange look great together. The Orient has given us jewel-brights like jade, sapphire, and ruby—striking when worn in combination. From India we have persimmon, saffron, and the curries to spice our wardrobes. These saturated colors, will enhance each other in offbeat ways, and look wonderfully new to our eyes.

Most women are still playing the fashion game by traditional rules. Don't be one of them. The dos and don'ts most of us grew up with no longer apply. There are no right or wrong colors, fashions, or hemlines. There are no hard-and-fast requirements for what to wear or when to wear it. Dressing today asks you to develop your own fashion sense. It means bringing *your* needs squarely to the fore. It means throwing out a lot of the old rules, as we've just done. The Lifestyle Wardrobe calls for a real turnaround in your fashion outlook. Just as taking a Lifestyle Inventory has helped you define your *real* clothing needs, forgetting the Fashion Myths will help you build a minimal wardrobe that gives you a maximum number of looks.

DRESSING TO SIZE: BIG AND BOLD

A large frame doesn't have to mean a big look. You can wear the lean line you see in fashion magazines rather than the loose look that is supposed to camouflage a fuller figure. Keep it simple and aim for a pulled-together look, but don't follow the same old rules.

- You don't have to wear jackets and tunics to conceal your figure.
- Slim, straight-leg pants don't make thighs look heavier.
- Lightweight fabrics cling and emphasize bulges; heavy-bodied fabrics stand away from the figure and conceal what's beneath.
- Narrow, hip-slung belts don't get lost on a large frame.
- Get rid of the notion that black is the only slenderizing color. Bright colors can be just as slim-looking and they make you feel good.
- Do wear knits. Just make sure you wear a no-cling slip underneath.
- Oversize accessories are fine, if they're kept in scale. If you're carrying a large bag, a shoulder strap can be slimming. A wide bangle on the wrist gives emphasis to your whole look.

DRESSING TO SIZE: PETITE NOT PRECIOUS

A petite frame needs clothes in the right scale but it doesn't call for cute little things. You *can* wear the bigger, bolder looks.

- Don't clutter up an outfit with small accessories. They look too busy.
- Handbags should be simple but not necessarily small. Teeny tiny handbags will look as though they were bought in the children's department.
- Big scarves and shawls won't overwhelm you; just make sure the colors blend with the rest of your outfit.
- One large, bulky piece of jewelry looks more important than small, neat pieces.
- Colored textured hose are fine on short legs. Wear them with the same color shoes for a leggy look.

M ost of us read about doing it. Some of us talk about doing it. A few of us actually do it. And those who do it at least once a year know that it pays off. Shopping in your own closet can be better than a clearance sale at your favorite store. You may see several bargains there you didn't think you'd ever locate. You could discover some fashion finds you never realized you owned. There may be a gold mine behind your closet door.

Getting a grip on your closet takes half a day. It will be less work than you think and more fun than you would have imagined. It just takes seeing your clothes with a different eye. And recognizing your own fashion image at the end is a reward in itself.

Here's how to shop in your own closet:

5. Shop in Your Own Closet

- Take everything out and divide it into five piles corresponding to the categories on your Lifestyle Chart.
    1. work
    2. dress-up
    3. casual/out
    4. casual/home
    5. active

- If you prefer not to use your bed or the floor, try hanging everything on a portable coat rack, the shower curtain rod, or a chinning bar.

- Wondering in which category to put a versatile turtleneck sweater, a classic silk shirt, or a pair of black pants? Perhaps you need a multifunctional group in addition to your "basic five." If something fits into more than three color designations it's a wardrobe staple—an item that can undergo a subtle but effective transformation depending upon what you wear it with. This group will most likely contain basic tops and bottoms—your beaded evening sweater or jogging pants don't belong here.

- Now look at your chart again. You'll see instantly whether your clothes synchronize with the blocks of color—what's lacking and where you own too much. You're going to be looking at the contents of your closet in a new way: not only from the point of view of current fashion and wearability but with your life in mind.

- Congratulate yourself on the groups of clothes that synchronize with your chart. If working is the largest block of color on your chart and the biggest pile you've made is daytime clothes that work along with you, give yourself a pat on the back for having recognized your lifestyle needs. But what about the categories where you own too many clothes or too few? If you own too few, you're obviously going to have to fill in the gap. If you own too many in one category, the pile will have to be thinned. But you don't have to throw out everything you own.

- Once you think you've hit on the one right look for you, you may decide to get rid of everything else you own. But the "right look" takes a while to achieve. You have to start, not with a "look," but with your lifestyle needs. By shopping with these needs in mind you *develop* your look. The lesson in all this? Don't weed out too fast.

- Don't think, "This shetland sweater belongs to another look which is no longer mine." There are ways you can change the sweater to suit your new image. If you've given up casual clothes for more tailored styles, wear the shetland under a suit, adding a white collar and pearls.

- If you've traded in a girlish look for a superefficient appearance, don't toss out the lace petticoats without considering this option: Wear them in layers under a flared tweed skirt.

- Maybe you're going in the other direction, deciding to have more fun with fashion. You suddenly hate the old-fashioned neutrals with which your closet seems to be overstocked. Don't discard them before you've asked yourself whether they could be used as background for streaks of color. Try buying some wit: a bright hairpick or set of combs, an elegant pocket handkerchief, a slinky, bright boa. Worn with strictly tailored styles or neutral colors, witty accessories stand out even more.

- Here's a surefire way to slim down the "fat" categories as well as the "mistakes" you haven't worn and don't know what to do with: REUSE, RETHINK, REVISE, RETIRE, REMOVE.

Keep what's wearable right now. *Reuse*

Invent a new way to wear what seems unwearable. For example, the black-and-white checked suit jacket that outlived its skirt can be rethought as a top for a solid black skirt or pants. Turn a two-piece shirt dress into a suit by wearing the top open, jacket-style, over a sweater or blouse. Or try other combinations—you may be surprised at what works now that never did before! *Rethink*

Transform tired items by redesigning them. Alterations are cheaper than buying new clothes. Chop a pair of full-length trousers to just above the knee, recuff them and you have a pair of Bermuda shorts. Jacket lapels can be narrowed or removed altogether and a worn cashmere sweater, cut off just below the armholes, can be made into a tube top. Or snip the ruffled collar from a dressy blouse and wear it at the neckline of a tailored dress or sweater. *Revise*

Retire   Set aside, either permanently or temporarily, anything you can't bear to part with—the clothes in which you've invested a lot, either financially or sentimentally, such as the dress you wore the night you met your husband or the designer jacket you treated yourself to on your first trip to Paris. Hold onto them, you might rethink or revise them later on, but keep them out of sight. Store them in a special see-through storage box under the bed or in an unused suitcase or in a portable closet in your basement or attic. This will free your closet of the unusables and yourself of guilt on seeing them.

Remove   Throw out the clothes that can't be reworn or redesigned. Fashion may be cyclical and styles do return but they never look the same way twice. Skirts may go thigh high again but they may not have the structured look of the 1960s.

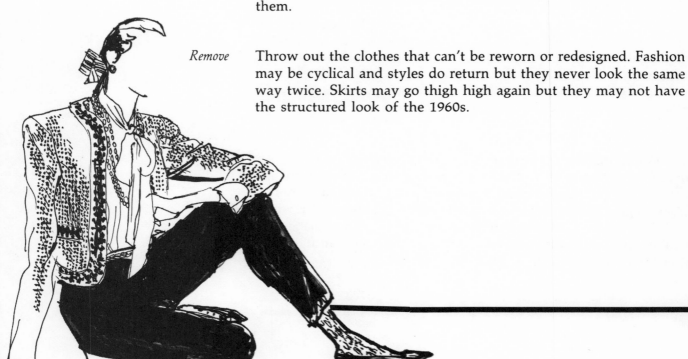

What you've got now is the core of your Lifestyle Wardrobe, the clothes that will work for the "basic five" areas on your chart. But don't close your closet door yet. Your clothes image is in there as well. Everything you need to know about your fashion image is right there in your closet.

How to find it? Analyze the clothes you feel secure in. Which are the pieces you always fall back on? Interview your wardrobe. Ask the winners some questions. Find out why the clothes that work for you do. The answers will give you the guidelines you'll need to complete your Lifestyle Wardrobe and give it a personal stamp.

1. Have I worn the item many times this season?

2. Do I feel particularly well dressed when I wear it?

3. Is this item something I can count on?

4. If I had it to do over, would I buy it again?

5. Would I be willing to buy it, or something like it, at a higher price?

You will most likely discover that the garments that rate a yes to all or most of these questions have certain elements in common:

- the same color or color family

- the same classification (suits, dresses, pants, skirts)

- the same general silhouette or shape

- the same style or look (tailored, soft, classic, trendy)

The fine line that runs through these pieces is your own special look.

Think about the outfits you feel best in. Are you a suit woman? Or a pants person? Are you a knit-dress lover? Do you feel most comfortable in a skirt and blouse? Or a shirtdress? What is it about them that makes you feel special? Next, visualize the clothes you disliked, which are now in the discard pile, and ask yourself why. Your answers will tell you a lot about your own best image.

"It's not me" means you may have bought someone else's image. Or the color may be wrong. It may look cheap. It never brings a compliment. It makes you feel unattractive or uncomfortable. Just as the winners in your closet are telling you what styles are best for you, the losers are telling you what to pass by.

How to tell a winner from a loser? It's as simple as two words: frequent use. If something is off its hanger a lot, it's a winner. If it just sits there, it's a loser.

But you can learn a lot from losers. Look at them, listen to them. What's *wrong* with clothes that spend their lives in the closet? You may have a whole list of complaints. The color that looked good in the store turns you green in daylight. You can't afford any more dry-cleaning bills for the white satin pajamas that seem to attract wine stains at every party. You don't have the time to iron that linen suit after every wearing. The gray jersey—you dutifully march off to work in it every few weeks because it was expensive —always makes you feel sad. The empire line has always been wrong for you but you couldn't resist that velvet dress that raises your waist to somewhere just below your armpits. The red cotton jumpsuit is "too much" for the office, and right now you have no big-time casual occasions in sight.

Booby traps, the lot of them! Or are they? Before you throw them out, make a mental note, or better yet, a *written* note, and paste it on your closet door. It might read:

No more

- turquoise
- white satin
- linen for work
- gray jersey
- empire-style dresses
- "fun" clothes

unless my life changes!

Obviously, learning how to avoid these mistakes will save you time and money. But there's more to it than that. Once the mistakes are out of your closet for good, you'll have room for clothes that can share the work load with your "old dependables."

It takes know-how to spot potential losers while they're still safely in the store. It pays to learn—and practice—how to do it. That way you can put your money on a winner every time.

The information you've gained from shopping in your own closet can be used as a guide to all future buying. What your closet shows you in the way of clothes preferences is your key to building a personal style. What the size of your "basic five" groups shows you about your clothing needs is your key to building a Lifestyle Wardrobe.

6. Building a Lifestyle Wardrobe

There are no success wardrobes but there *are* successful wardrobe systems. Notice the plural here: There is more than just one way of building a Lifestyle Wardrobe. Consider these options:

THE SUIT ALTERNATIVE

For the first time in American history, more women are working outside the home than are staying in it. Today, only about one-third of adult women are full-time homemakers. Another 15 percent are women who work part-time, are retired, or attend school. The rest—more than 52 percent —are in the labor force. The "Success Suit" evolved from this un- precedented change in women's lives. It was a fashion designed to ease them painlessly into the world of men. However, women soon realized that the three-piece beige uniform that made them fade into the background also made them fade from sight when promo- tions were being passed around.

Today most women are feeling much more comfortable with their roles as business and professional women. Career dressing no longer means drab colors and three-piece gabardine. However, some fields still require a suited image. But a suited look can also mean:

- Strict man-tailoring softened by feminine additions: a pinstripe suit worn with a soft, ruffled blouse, lace pocket handkerchief, or flower and pearls.

- The unmatched suit: solid skirt and patterned top.

- The knit suit, either matched or unmatched, worn with or without a blouse.

- A well-tailored pantsuit.

Women in top positions can be individuals when it comes to fashion. We interviewed several women executives. Here's a sampling of their views:

Program officer in the educational division of one of the largest nonprofit organizations in the United States. Terry wears a black linen designer dress of austere simplicity. On a hook behind her office door hangs its elegant beige jacket. And on her feet are a racy pair of bright red kid sling-back shoes.

Terry S.

"I adore shoes. They're my weakness, I suppose. Everybody knows about it. My friends call me up and say, 'I just saw the most terrific pair of "Terry" shoes in that little shop on Madison Avenue' and I have to run right over. That's how I shop. Shoes are my trademark.

"I've thought about clothes a lot. Note, I said *thought.* Because I just don't have time to think about how I look constantly. When I came to this job I planned my wardrobe the way I would plan out a new educational project. Pencil, paper, and all. It paid off—now I don't think about it anymore.

"The result of my planning is sets of work ensembles. Black, beige, and red. It's as simple as that. And I don't have a single print in my wardrobe. When I planned my dressing strategy I knew I was talking about a lot of money. I also knew that in my office, suits were going to be the rule. Now, there's been a lot of nonsense about the 'power suit,' about dressing for success. No one knows better than I that the professional world has its rules about dress. But I also know better than anyone else about the professional *me,* and I wasn't about to be pushed into some timid three-piece gabardine suit!

"I'm five feet seven inches tall, and I can wear very large expanses of bright color since I'm dark haired. So I thought: I love red.

What goes best with red? What can I play it off against? And I came up with black and beige, which also complement each other—and me—very well.

"I decided that red was my color, and shoes my favorite indulgence. If I put my money on those two categories, I couldn't go wrong. I knew I couldn't be wallflowerish about style with my height and coloring, so I made the decision right then and there: no prints. Just bold jewelry and lots of wonderful shoes. It's worked, I'm glad to say."

TERRY'S FASHION PHILOSOPHY: "Once you know that a strong sense of yourself is your best power tool, it becomes easier to reveal yourself in the way you dress. Your 'look' should seem to transcend what you wear, though you use clothes to achieve it. To give my 'audience' something to identify me by, I repeat it until it's mine. That's when people start calling me about seeing 'my' shoes in stores. But it can be anything as long as it's yours: a fresh daisy in your lapel, a stock tie in a sizzling silk, one for each suit—and gloves to match. These may flaunt the rule book, but what woman ever got ahead by looking anonymous?"

Susan H.   Managing editor of a national monthly magazine. A self-confessed exercise nut, her sports don't suffer because of her job. She has classic American good looks—the kind of perfect-featured blonde healthiness we all envy. Her wardrobe is a lot more casual than Terry's, and she manages to incorporate her activewear right into it, making the sports-look her trademark.

"But I still have to deal with the suit problem. After all, I can't appear at a Monday morning staff meeting in riding clothes or my tennis whites. Okay, I thought, what do I do when I come to work after my early morning ride in the park? Where do I change? It may sound like a special sort of situation, but I'll bet there are a lot of women who are spending at least their lunch hour at an exercise class. So the question is: what do you do with the leotard? I answered that one long ago. I've been wearing leotards under everything I own for ages.

44

"What do I do about suits? It's easy. I've developed my 'un-matched-suit' system. My riding jacket is a beigy-brown tweed. I keep one beige corduroy skirt and a pair of pumps at the office all the time. After my once-a-week ride in the park, I whip into the ladies' room, sponge off, remove my jodphurs and boots, and put on the skirt and shoes. I'm ready for meetings, author interviews, whatever.

"What do I wear under my riding jacket? My stock-tie shirt in summer, a turtleneck in winter. Both look right with my 'un-matched suit.' The most important thing is planning ahead according to your needs. The reason I wear a leotard under everything, all the time, is that I might just want to shed some tension after work, so I'll take a jazz class. I'm never unprepared. And if an invitation for dinner and dancing comes up after a late day at the office—well, with my bare leotard and an evening skirt—I'm equipped for the event!"

SUSAN'S FASHION PHILOSOPHY: "Think it out. Be prepared."

Lawyer in a large law firm.   *Ann D.*

"I'm in court a lot and a suit is what they expect you to wear. So I decided early that if I can't buck the suit system, I'd substitute my own strategy: I'd use suits as a sort of neutral background for my personal signature.

"I feel this way about it: In work like mine, you have to project your best self, the self you want your client and colleagues to see. Too often, women on the way up duck behind 'correct' dress. They use the suit as camouflage. What this says about them is that they are running scared, or, at the very least, that they are intimidated by their surroundings or their responsibilities. To my way of thinking, a suit is no place to hide!

"I've discovered a way to make suits work to my advantage. My problem was how to avoid a too-strict appearance: that's a trap women lawyers often fall into. I don't want to look like my twelfth grade math teacher or the librarian with her hair in a bun. So instead, I decided to amuse myself with the suit look. If I'm going

45

to be in a suit, I felt I might as well be comfortable and have fun. There aren't any laws against *that*—not even in court. So I hit on my version of the 'look.' Now, I know that all the 'success' books tell you to cut your hair to medium length, wear neutral colors, and avoid long, painted nails. I have hair a yard long and I wear it loose. I polish my nails. I wear every tone of pink and mauve and fuchsia I can get my hands on. And another thing: I have initials embroidered on the cuffs of every shirt I own." An individual trademark for sure.

ANN'S FASHION PHILOSOPHY: "The first thing about all clothes is that they talk. You have to take a close look at the suit to see what it communicates. The suit announces 'competence' to the world around you. To you personally it also says 'convenience' and 'comfort.' Worn as a whole, the suit looks polished; worn as separates, its pieces give you a variety of options. Suits offer the best solution to the three biggest shopping problems facing a busy woman: lack of time, the bewilderment of too much choice, and inflationary costs. That's my commercial for the suit; it really is the best dress option for work.

"Once you know that clothes talk, you have to ask yourself the big question: What do I want my clothes to say? Your aim should be to present a coherent image, one that repeats your 'note' in a memorable way. Now, that's the fun of a suit—it gives you a background against which to work. It's all up to you. I moderate a very mannish suit with a long silk scarf tied in a floppy bow at the throat. And I sharpen a suit with a fedora, seamed stockings, and gloves. Try it out, it could become your trademark. I remember Oscar Wilde's advice: 'Only superficial people refuse to judge by appearances.' Since your associates should and do take seriously how you look, they might as well be looking at the best you. So I wear my suits with a difference. And I have fun with them!"

Kathleen M.   is vice-president and partner-to-be at one of the most prestigious investment banking firms in the country. She appears on the floor of the stock exchange in—surprise!—an extremely floaty flower-printed dress.

"I know that I hold a very high position on the 'success-ladder' but I look awful in anything tailored. I adore dresses. *They're* my signature. I must have three dozen!

KATHLEEN'S FASHION PHILOSOPHY: "I'll be honest. I don't have to dress for success. I feel I'm already there."

Talking with these women started us thinking about some other suit alternatives:

I f you're not the suit type, or your figure is wrong for man-tailoring, you have a world of less tailored choices at your disposal:

THE SOFT DRESSING STRATEGY

- dresses, soft skirts, silk blouses, unconstructed jackets, sweater jackets

These will give you a wardrobe which, though untailored in manner, is right for your style and just as correct as a suit for an office or working life.

I f work or recreation finds you often in trains or planes, the way to go is with knits. Sweater or jersey knits which require no ironing, little maintenance, and tend to be seasonless should be the basis of your wardrobe. This way, almost every piece you own can be rolled to pack uncrushably.

GOING WITH KNITS

Having a full figure shouldn't keep you from wearing knits. After all, large women travel just as often as their smaller sisters. So let's put that old myth about "no knits above size 12" to rest right away. Try an all-in-one body suit underneath a knit dress. Presto! Not a bulge in sight. Under knit pants, wear sheer pantyhose. Further advice about clinging: keep a can of antistatic spray on hand.

THE UNIFORM OPTION

If you know yourself well and have established a confident clothes image, if your life has a fixed pattern, you've already narrowed your options. Buying in multiples is your best bet, once you know what's for you. For example, the woman who looks *best* in a suit and *needs* a tailored image for her work life would do well to listen to designer Oscar de la Renta: "A woman who works has got to have a professional, no-nonsense attitude—a kind of uniform—the equivalent of a man's gray flannel suit."

For this woman, suits are her uniform. For a different kind of lifestyle, turtleneck sweaters and matching pants or skirts could be the uniform. Another woman might choose to live in shirtdresses or knit pantsuits. It's a matter of making the decision to narrow your own style options to what works for your life, and then wearing it over and over.

CASUAL-CHIC

This wardrobe alternative is for women for whom career doesn't mean "office," or for women who work in an industry with a free-wheeling dress code. A casual-chic wardrobe affords many advantages: There's more room for inventiveness and flexibility when the only image you have to worry about is your own, not the corporation's.

The wardrobe-wise know there's more than one way to build your own version of the Lifestyle Wardrobe: It can include anything from jeans and jumpsuits to caftans and warmups. It's your casual wardrobe "working" in yet another way.

Halston's clothes philosopy hinges on the less-is-best approach. *Less Is Best*
Fewer colors and fewer pieces, according to the designer, make for
maximum versatility. "I think it's better to have a limited wardrobe
with different component parts," he says, "so that you can have as
many changes as possible. It requires pieces: a one-piece dress, a
skirt with blouses, a suit, a separate jacket. And then some sweater
dressing. I think the secret is to limit the colors."

One elegant outfit or a closet full of new clothes: Either is possible *Best Can Be Most*
for about the same outlay of money. Sometimes the "big splurge"
can deliver the most pow. When you spend your entire budget on
one wonderful item that blows your mind every time you wear it
—and you wear it often—your money's been well spent.

There are times, however, when putting your entire clothes budget *More Can Be Best*
into a few expensive pieces just doesn't give you your money's
worth. One elegant outfit can make you feel terrific, but it can't
substitute for a wardrobe that will take you from car pool to volunteer job, to making dinner, to an evening out. If *that's* what you need,
several less expensive separates *can* be best.

And, on the subject of money, there are two approaches to
Investment Dressing. First there's:

LONG-TERM INVESTMENT: We all recognize these items. They're clothes
of great quality, exquisite workmanship and fabric. Classics with a
track record, guaranteed to last. They could be a furlined trenchcoat,
a suede hacking jacket, a little black dress, a tweed skirt, a silk
blouse. They're usually expensive but we buy them because they'll
pay back their initial cost by years of wear.

Yves St. Laurent talks about limiting the components of a modern wardrobe. "A woman should build her wardrobe as a man does—with clothes that are timeless, give her confidence, and never make her feel démodé . . . A woman's wardrobe should not change every six months. She should be able to wear the pieces she already owns and add to them. They should be like timeless classics."

But there's another kind of clothes buy that pays its way equally well. It's called the:

SHORT-TERM INVESTMENT: This is the outfit you buy because it's trendy and right in style. You wear it to death *that very season* and it's just as cost-effective as an item you wear less frequently but over a longer period of time.

Here's where it's smart to think of clothes as a *tool*.

DEBORAH S., after eighteen months in a consulting firm, is gunning for the position of program director. She's impatient, but the time is right: she can't afford to miss the opportunity. An image change is one of her first priorities since she needs to give a "visual nudge" to her superiors. She wants to be thought of in a new way. She wants to be noticed. And it doesn't take a genius to figure out that in the world of business, the image is the message.

What does Deborah S. do? She repackages herself for the position she's aiming for. Dressing "up" we call it. She's willing to step out of her former image and take a chance on her new one. How? She begins to appear at work in some dashing new clothes. A bright red suit, a less expensive copy of this season's Halston; a Perry Ellis sweater look-alike; a sophisticated khaki, white, and red color scheme.

Little money, big results: Deborah S. got a lot of mileage from her new purchases. Never mind that she had bought copies of this season's designer hits; she knew what she was doing. She reasoned that you can't look successful if you look dated. Clothes are a tool you can learn to use like any other method of getting ahead. Deborah's short-term investment paid off in long-term results.

A good clothes investment should never be calculated only on the basis of the number of years you happen to own something. Investment dressing is based on effectiveness as well as on the number of wearings you get from your clothes.

7. The Sum of the Parts

The whole is greater than the sum of the parts. That theory is just as sound in wardrobe planning as it is in mathematics. And nowhere is the theory of synergism more important than in a Lifestyle Wardrobe where each piece is a key component rather than a random part; where each piece moves from day to day, from outfit to outfit, expanding your wardrobe and your fashion alternatives.

Expandables are adaptable clothes that aren't locked into being worn in only one way. They work alone and with each other. They mix with a new item or with the clothes you already own and they never look the same way twice. Expandables are blouses, shirts, skirts, jackets, sweaters, pants, dresses, coats. They can be classics or the latest styles. They can be anything as long as they're versatile.

You could build a whole Lifestyle Wardrobe around one beautiful jacket. A braid-trimmed, Chanel-type cardigan, perhaps the surviving piece of a suit, could be a key Expandable:

- over a ruffled chiffon blouse with a velvet skirt
- over a silk camisole and matching silk pants
- over a printed shirt dress
- over a tweed skirt and turtleneck sweater
- over gabardine pants with a silk shirt
- over jeans

Or take the beautiful lace blouse you bought for a special occasion and haven't worn since. It could be worn:

- with a tailored suit
- as a jacket over a silk camisole and matching silk pants
- as a jacket over a dressy dress
- as a coverup for a bare evening dress

These pieces are key Expandables. Think "expandable" and see if you don't come up with one or two of your own. All it requires is looking at what you already have, assigning it additional roles—and then making multiple demands on what you buy. Expandables in action are money savers! For clothes that give you the most for your money are those that work with everything else you own.

Calvin Klein has said it all: "Clothes today are expensive . . . so it's really important that all the pieces in a wardrobe work together. A successful woman needs clothes that are versatile, that give her lots of mileage, that she can mix with other pieces and wear lots of different ways. Every blouse and sweater and jacket should go with skirts, trousers, and jeans . . . should work dressed up or down depending on . . . how the pieces themselves are used."

There are two ingredients necessary in achieving the kind of wardrobe Calvin Klein is talking about:

1. Identifying and using key Expandables

2. Limiting your colors

Before you can make the sum of these Expandables add up to more than the parts, you must learn how to color-limit your wardrobe. This ensures that every part works with every other.

Yves St. Laurent illustrates this point in almost every collection. He will put together a white wool pantsuit, white silk blouse, white silk scarf and move his pieces into combinations with a black jacket, black camisole, black pants. Seven pieces, triple the number of looks. That's Expandable know-how.

YSL is able to get this kind of interchangeability by working with very few parts and using only black and white. But don't for a moment imagine that you have to be limited to only two colors. Wardrobe minimalism can be achieved equally well with three or four colors and can be just as dramatic when it's carried out with several tones of a single color. Monochromatic, as you'll see in the next chapter, can be anything but dull!

How does the Expandables concept translate into a wardrobe when your Lifestyle Chart is mostly green for work? If your focus is on your career, if you spend most of your time in an office, if you need clothes that go from work to a cocktail reception or dinner, if you're beginning to travel for business and need a wardrobe that can face climate changes, you'll need component parts that will give you as many changes as possible for the five business days of the week. A lot to expect? Those demands can be met thanks to Expandables.

Key Expandable for a working wardrobe: a double-faced wool coat or cape in charcoal and banker's gray. The trick: Carry those two colors throughout your other pieces. Add a gray jacket, skirt, and pants in matching fabric. Vary with black and cream: a silk shirt, a ribbed turtleneck, a dramatic shawl. Now you have a seven-piece wardrobe in which each part acts as an Expandable, working with every other part and giving you outfit possibilities almost beyond count.

How does this Lifestyle Wardrobe travel? Perfectly, once you've edited it for your destination. The best travel wardrobe you can own is, quite simply, a pared-down version of the one you have. For example, you'll wear the coat, pants, and black sweater on the plane. For extra warmth, you can add the shawl. The pants, silk shirt, and shawl could go to dinner later on, and the jacket, pants, and silk shirt would be perfect for a client meeting the next morning.

If your multifaceted activities are home-based, the Expandables principle still applies. You may spend your day life—driving to your part-time job, picking up the children from school—in jeans or pantsuits. But, what if your night life demands clothes for evenings at restaurants, the country club, dinner parties, or entertaining at home? Does this mean a whole new wardrobe? Not necessarily.

Your daytime taupe wool pantsuit also has a night life. Remember the silk camisole and pants? They're part of a group of separates that also includes a matching jacket. And the lace blouse that doubles as a coverup? It too plays an important role in your evening life. Combine the pieces in this mini-wardrobe as you will: They'll take you anywhere, from little evenings at home to big evenings out.

The Expandables approach is the smartest way to go even if you work in a more casual environment. Some careers, in the arts or media, may allow for a less structured style, but you still want a maximum number of looks with a minimum number of pieces. If your Lifestyle Chart shows green for work, blue for casual-out, and yellow for casual-home in almost equal balance, if your career takes you from one assignment to another, the demands on your clothes are enormous. But your eclectic taste and the fun you have dressing with Expandables will get you through the variety of situations you must meet.

One imaginative item—a multicolored three-quarter-length sweater coat, is your key Expandable. Everything in your wardrobe —casual sportswear, the ethnic dresses you love, and the distinctive separates you collect—repeats one or more colors of your coat. This means that each piece works with every other piece using the coat as a catalyst as well as an Expandable. Your wardrobe even spans the temperature changes some of your business trips entail. You've picked your fabrics carefully and by avoiding extraheavy, hairy fabrics and very lightweight, flimsy fabrics you can layer your clothes and be comfortable in most climates.

Expandables work whether your budget is tight or infinite. The principle remains the same: Everything works with everything else, giving you more options than you ever thought possible. How? By combining the pieces over and over in different ways. And why not?

JANUARY	MAY	SEPTEMBER
Lingerie	Dresses	
Cosmetics	Lingerie	
Jewelry		
Holiday clothes		
FEBRUARY	**JUNE**	**OCTOBER**
Winter clothes	Summer clothes	Coats
Shoes	Shoes	Handbags
Skiwear		Fall sportswear
MARCH	**JULY**	**NOVEMBER**
Boots	Bathing suits	Fall clothes
Furs	Beachwear	
	Cosmetics	
APRIL	**AUGUST**	**DECEMBER**
Spring clothes	Furs	Sweaters
		Accessories
		Lingerie

They're switchable, which makes them much more than coordinates. By working together they stretch your wardrobe and your clothing dollars beyond what each could do alone—proving that the whole is greater than the sum of the parts.

Fashion minimalism isn't just for the budget-minded. You may want to own fewer but more expensive clothes and knowing they're Expandables takes the sting out of spending. They will pay you well no matter what your clothing budget. Just remember the cardinal rule: Each piece you add must go with the clothes you already own.

Each piece should expand your wardrobe by *more* than just one option. Think numbers. Think sum of the parts. And get used to looking at clothes with this question in mind: Is this item going to increase my options? It won't take you long to develop a flair for tracking down the Expandables you need. And once you've learned how the Continuous Color Concept sets Expandables to work, you'll never again go back to buying random parts.

T he trick to making Expandables work is color. Color is one of the most delicious basics of life. Don't let outworn rules about color spoil your fun. Trust your instinct when you choose the colors for your Lifestyle Wardrobe.

Choice of color should be personal. Don't allow yourself to be hemmed in by directions like these: redheads look best in green; olive complexions can't wear black; blondes should stick to pastels. Color-typing is a common mistake. We all tend to acquire "mindsets" about what we can and can't wear. Where would Lucille Ball and Arlene Dahl be without red to put themselves over? Can you imagine Lena Horne in anything besides slinky black? Tuesday Weld likes herself best in a dark leotard—none of the candy-box pastels for her! Tawny-complexioned Ali

McGraw says, "I have a lot of black . . . and earth colors. Most of my clothing seems to be brown, beige, black, and cream-colored." The truth is that redheads look sensational in reds and pinks. Dark complexions need only use a more translucent makeup, which reflects color rather than absorbs it, to look terrific in black. And no one looks better in dark shades than a blonde.

The only valid rule is: Choose colors that really speak to you. You'll love your clothes all the more and you won't waste money on something you thought you had to have because it's the latest color. Don't be concerned if khaki is the fashion color of the current season and green is "out." If green is your color, track it down, but look for a green that's muted—more toward khaki than emerald or parrot green. You *can* have your best color in a current version. Old colors never die—each season will bring a variation of your favorite.

For there *are* trends in colors. Teal or fuchsia will—like a fashion fad itself—come in strong one season and go out with the next. Curry, chamois, persimmon, chestnut—will these be the next rage?

Without doubt the American color sense has become more and more sophisticated as we travel and as our technology for reproducing color on fabric improves, exposing us to an ever wider range of shades. Remember when we brought the brilliant reds, pinks, and oranges of Latin America back home? We had never seen such saturated brights before. They were vegetable dyes but we found a way to reproduce them here. More recently we've seen the soft Icelandic colors—grays, beiges, and browns—worn together. A color's origins give it character: Biba, one of the English designers of the Mod era, introduced muddy pre-Raphaelite shades from England in the early 1970s; recently the sun-baked, desert colors of our own Southwest have been in vogue.

Colors have *aura,* too. Some colors talk "shy" (pale pink, baby blue), some say "bold" (chrome yellow, electric blue, orange), some are sophisticated (navy, gray, black), some look out-and-out expensive (camel, pearl gray, creamy beige, off-white). Yes, there *is* a color caste system.

There are lots of reasons you have "favorites." We've all grown up with tastes we can't explain. The quality of light in our climate, exposure to other countries and cultures, associations with objects, early memories. All these play a part. But whatever your color preferences, the point is to be aware of them. Keep a mental inventory. There's something instinctive at work when a color reaches right out and grabs your eye, whether it's in a painting, in nature, on the racks in a department store, or in your own closet. Let it happen and use that color in your Lifestyle Wardrobe. Use it even if some chart says it's not supposed to flatter your skin type. You've seen how unreliable and outmoded the supposed-tos are. Your own instincts will pay off in the end: You'll find yourself living in the colors you really love.

When you sound out your color preferences, here's something to keep in mind: You've been taught to think of colors as "warm" —red and yellow and all the variations in between—and "cool"— blue and green in all their guises. But there's another way of looking at color, one that gives you a much wider field of choice in picking your favorites. All colors begin with the three primaries: red, blue, and yellow. All other colors are secondaries, that is, combinations of these. Value and intensity are what make for the myriad of colors we see.

Intensity is a much more intelligent way to approach color. Instead of thinking "favorite shade" think "favorite intensity." Perhaps you like the whole range of darks: stone gray, taupe, ochre, olive, teal, and burgundy. Now lighten them to dove gray, lemon, sand, mint green, baby blue, pink. Do they still have the same appeal? It's *intensity* that determines your color choices as well as the color itself. Recognizing your preference for certain intensities as well as hues will widen your options—even in a narrow color range.

Turning up the volume on your favorite color can also give you a "bright." Brights are fully saturated basic colors. Their chroma, or degree of brilliance, seems lit from behind. Think of stop-light colors: fire-engine red, school-bus yellow, emerald green. Brights can be royal blue, orange, or crimson as well.

BRIGHTS: primary and secondary colors in full intensity—hot bursts of crayon colors, full of light and life

SOFT, MID-TONE BRIGHTS: lively, jewel colors, floral colors, exotic but gentle

PALE PASTELS: palest blushes of primary and secondary brights

NATURAL PALES: soft, subtle, barely there, go-with-everything neutrals that also work alone

RICH TAPESTRY COLORS: intense, sophisticated vegetable dyes

DEEP DARK: saturated, strong, dark neutrals

What makes your color choice work in the Lifestyle Wardrobe is knowing how to *limit* it and use it in a Continuous Color Concept. The Continuous Color Concept offers the fastest way of pulling a wardrobe together visually. It means choosing a single color or color group for all your Expandables. In this way, color becomes the catalyst that allows your Expandables to group and regroup; it literally holds your Lifestyle Wardrobe together.

Having a Continuous Color Concept increases your wardrobe substantively. Each piece works with every other piece and you're limited only by your imagination —not by the pieces themselves. Having a variety of colors in your wardrobe doesn't increase the number of looks or outfits. It decreases them because nothing works with anything else.

The previous chapter outlined three wardrobe systems using Expandables—now let's fill in the outlines with color. There are three basic ways of using the Continuous Color Concept to hold your wardrobe together.

THE MONOCHROMATIC COLOR SCHEME

This is the easiest, the most foolproof scheme, and has the most impact. Nothing is more effective than one-color dressing—either for a whole wardrobe or a single outfit. There are some colors that work especially well in a monochromatic strategy. Their intensity is listed from pale to dark:

- lilac — mauve — violet — purple
- oatmeal — beige — taupe — espresso
- pearl gray — medium gray — banker's gray — charcoal
- cream — sand — camel — brown

A second method of limiting your color scheme is with a shot of color.

SHOT-OF-COLOR
STRATEGY

hoose a basic neutral combination like black and white or beige and brown, and spark it with one witty color. This can be eye-catching if the accent color is bright:

- black pants, white blazer, *red* shirt

  or subtle if the shot-of-color is dark:
- brown tweed suit, *curry* sweater

  and quietly effective with a pale shade:
- burnt orange dress, *lemon yellow* scarf

The best-dressed corporate wife we know wore red, white, and blue for years. "I grew tired of looking like a flag," she confides, "but navy is such a good color for me. And I own so many navy and white basics." She now sharpens her standbys with buttercup yellow and dusty rose accents for a newer, more sophisticated look that's still "me."

Interior decorators will often design a room based on *Variations on a Print,* a floral fabric or a painting or a striped or geometric pattern containing all the colors they will later single out to use as solids. A red, white, and blue room can evolve from a Calder painting, a peach and dove gray room from a Chinese print. You can build your wardrobe using the same principle: pulling solid colors from a print or multicolor Expandable. Each piece will work with the print or with one another:

- a wine/forest green/purple/rust-striped two-piece knit dress can be the catalyst for a group of wine, forest green, and rust Expandables

- a slate/terra-cotta/mustard paisley print shawl ties together a wardrobe of these three outstanding colors

The important thing to remember about showing your colors is that they're seasonless. Your dark Expandables don't have to spend the summer in mothballs and your pastel pieces will look just as right in a colder climate. Today all colors are season spanners: it's a modern approach that applies to fabrics, too.

We know a woman who sends out the same color message at every public appearance she makes: a luxurious shade of creamy, golden-beige. Her own hair color dictated this choice and the effect is dramatic. The irony is that her audience is never bored even though they know what to expect. She'll be in beige, of course, so eyes focus on the line and fabric of her clothes. But the major focus is—you guessed it—on her.

A friend, reentering the work force after many years of raising a family, has put together a career wardrobe of four classic colors: black, white, charcoal, and camel. This way all her separates work well with each other. "I don't own one piece that won't go with everything else in my wardrobe, including my white coat," she said, then confided, "It simplifies shopping—I just don't have to look at any other color, no matter how tempting it may be. It's a relief to have fewer options!"

BLACK: VARIATIONS ON A THEME

PALOMA PICASSO: "My three favorite colors are black, white, and red. But, of course, I deviate from that . . . I dress very often in bright colors, but it's always with black and one other bright."

DONNA KARAN, designer: "Three years ago a woman could get away with a pair of good black pants, a good black skirt, black turtleneck, a pair of boots in a neutral color, straight-leg jeans, and a fabulous belt." _Note:_ she still can. Some things never change—especially the elegance of black.

DIANA VREELAND's classic winter uniform: "Three black cashmere sweaters rotated with three black Givenchy skirts."

INGEBORG DAY, writer: "In the winter I wear black. Two pairs of black pants, a black skirt, a black wool turtleneck, a fisherman's sweater, and a short-sleeve black sweater. I have a pair of black evening sandals and Italian boots."

LYNN CAINE, author: "I think a woman goes through color stages the way she goes through life stages. In my twenties I wore lots of black to set off my black hair. Then I went through a blue-green period —I felt it played up my green eyes. Finally, a friend who knows about clothes said to me, 'You should be wearing purples.' And she was right. Now I have the whole plum-mauve-violet spectrum to choose from. Sometimes it takes an expert's eye. It's hard to know yourself colorwise."

9. The Right Goods

Designers talk about seasonless dressing but go right on turning out four different collections a year. Department stores continue to advertise transseasonal clothes and do so four times a year. Everybody's talking "seasonless" but nobody's doing it. Or so it seems. But you *can* put together a truly seasonless Lifestyle Wardrobe using what's available at any time of the year, if you know what fabrics to look for.

Many designers say their fabrics span the seasons. It's true that anything from thin suede to batiste can be adapted to almost any climate with a little stretch of ingenuity. But that's not the point! Transseasonal fabrics don't need to be "adapted"—they need only be worn twelve months of the year. How do you know when something's truly transseasonal? You don't store it away—*ever*.

There are several reasons to own as many clothes as possible in seasonless fabrics. Today women travel more and need a variety of pieces that can go anywhere, to any climate. With seasonless dressing you can take six or seven Expandables and travel the world over—summer or winter. Seasonless dressing makes life easier: There's no reason to buy two items when one will do. It shouldn't be necessary to change your complete wardrobe each season. For example, a silk cardigan will give you more mileage than one in very heavy wool or very lightweight cotton.

Which fabrics *really* deliver on the promise of all-year-round wear?

- silk knit jersey
- silk crepe de chine
- silk sweater-knit
- wool jersey
- wool crepe
- cotton knit
- denim
- velours
- synthetic and rayon blends

Weight more than fiber content determines seasonlessness. Remember that the lightweight versions of heavy fabrics and the heavy types of lightweight fabrics always look right regardless of the time and temperature.

Precisely because you'll be wearing your seasonless fabrics all year round, you'll want them to have all the surface interest and texture that our sophisticated modern fabric technology can supply. **Texture** gives fabric its character and variety. It keeps all fabrics from looking alike and the eye from being bored. What could be more witty than sweatshirt fabric piped in gold for evening? And satin running shorts are already a familiar sight by day.

Texture, more than style or color, can make your clothes look rich. Texture actually determines the "feel" of a color on the fabric. Every color does not work in every fabric. Notice that paler colors look more important in rich textures whereas deep colors give weight to thin, more fluid fabrics. A woman dressed all in white, without any texture, can look as if she's wearing a nurse's uniform after hours. Now, picture that same woman with white flannel trousers, white damask blouse, and white mohair cardigan. Our woman in white has turned from a duckling to a swan—courtesy of texture.

"GOODS" CARE

Creme-Rinse your woolens: a capful in the final rinse water will act as a fabric softener.

Iron your newly washed sweaters on the reverse side to prevent stiffening.

Ammonia (2 capfuls) added to the wash water eliminates yellowing from white or pale beige wools.

An Electric Shaver removes pilling from sweaters.

Wet and freeze pantyhose before the first wearing—they'll last longer.

Refrigerate your angora sweaters to prevent shedding.

Salt your sweat away: 4 tablespoons in a quart of water freshens active sportswear.

Screen your sweater dry. Spread it over a clean window screen placed over the bathtub or sink. A hair dryer will speed the process.

Think of how artists use texture to vary their paintings. They use impasto applied with a palette knife; they drip, spatter, and splotch the paint; they use collage. You can do the same thing if you think of your wardrobe as a canvas. And the most dramatic example is the monochromatic scheme. Picture the pearl-to-charcoal-gray career wardrobe in a variety of weaves. With texture it's transformed from serviceable to sophisticated.

10. Addables: Making Clothes Talk

SCENE

A business lunch in Milan. An Italian executive mentions to her American counterpart a company she's doing business with in the States.

AMERICAN: Then you know the vice president, DK?

ITALIAN: Of course I know DK, the woman with the marvelous belt!

AMERICAN: That belt is her trademark. She's almost as well known for it as she is for her ability.

ITALIAN: It's interesting how an accessory like that belt can stay in your mind, no?

AMERICAN: Ah, but it's not an "accessory" for DK—it's clothes. It's the way she dresses.

No, there's no such thing as an accessory! In a Lifestyle Wardrobe there's no room for two separate categories of clothing. It's foolish to think about "garments" on the one hand and "accessories" on the other, as though the latter were there only to decorate what you wear. Each item in your Lifestyle Wardrobe is an Expandable that works with every other piece—and that includes "accessories." It's time to let them share billing as major items. Let's call them Addables and give them equal rights and equal responsibilities with your other clothes. That means they have to be measured by the same yardstick as any other Expandable—the Lifestyle Chart.

ITALIAN.   That belt must have cost a fortune—it's enormous. It's sterling silver, no?

AMERICAN.   She's had it for years and she'll probably wear it forever. She wears it with the simplest skirts and pants and sweaters—so maybe she's really *saving* a fortune.

That's another reason why Addables are in the big league now: money. At today's prices, boots and belts and bags can represent as much of an investment as a suit or a coat, except that they're likely to stay in fashion—and in use—longer. And if they're obviously expensive, they can make less expensive clothes look "rich."

Addables must have *impact.* Don't fall into the trap of thinking about them as wonderful "little" items—the kind you fall in love with, pay a pretty price for, and watch spending their lives on your shelves. That can't happen if you apply the Lifestyle Principle to *everything* you buy—suits or shoes and handbags—and if you buy only important pieces. When it comes to Addables the trick is to pare down; numbers won't give you points. DK's belt eliminates the need for a whole wardrobe of belts.

To prove that Addables aren't "extras," think of a multicolor convertible clutch bag. If it's in the same color scheme that runs right through your closet, it can work as a pivotal point in your wardrobe—a unifier rather than a mere accessory.

The cardinal rules with Addables, as with Expandables, are: Does my lifestyle require it? Will it work with everything in my wardrobe? And, does it look important?

The multicolor clutch may be the perfect bag for you if you live an office life and can slip it into your attaché case. It may be less than perfect if yours is a free-lance career and most of your office has to be carried along with you. But there's a handbag for every woman's life, from canvas tote to runner's pouch. In fact, have you ever stopped to think that you can tell what a woman does by the handbag she carries? In other words, Addables talk—LOUD.

Just remember: Although your Addables can say a lot about you, they can't do everything for you. We've all read those clever magazine articles that show how one scarf can change a dress seven different ways or take a suit from dawn to disco—in brief—make a silk purse from a sow's ear. Nonsense! A scarf can't transform one dress into another. Now, it's true that a colorful scarf will make the dress look more festive, but that alone won't take you out dancing. In fact, on the wrong dress it can make you look just plain silly. Addables aren't really wardrobe stretchers; they're catalysts that hold the pieces together.

Here are some of the magical things Addables *can* do if you use them the same way you've learned to use your other Expandables.

HANDBAGS

Take ~~the~~ *a* multicolor handbag. With one pair of shoes or boots for each color, you've eliminated the need for any other handbag and quadrupled the wearability of this one. ~~That's what's meant by using an Addable like an Expandable.~~

Accessory

Next to a multicolor handbag, a neutral color bag is an excellent ~~Addable~~. But don't judge today's neutrals by yesterday's definition. The accessory colors to look for aren't the safe, supposedly go-with-everything colors like brown, black, or navy. They're violet or turquoise or red or fuchsia or green—neutral colors because they behave in a completely versatile manner—increasing the number of ways you can wear them. And they do more than "go-with." They're like vitamins—energizers—to give your wardrobe vitality that the old-style neutrals couldn't produce.

Multicolor or neutral, the most adaptable handbag to own is a convertible clutch: a basic large or small clutch with a removable shoulder strap. With its strap, it's suitable for almost any casual occasion and without it can go anywhere from office to dinner. Remember, any handbag, regardless of the color, deserves two or three pairs of matching or coordinating footwear. Pumps, casual walking shoes, and boots, for example, will take the same handbag anywhere, day or evening.

SHOES

Shoe styles change faster than any other ~~Addables~~ *accessory*. However, they can be money-stretchers if you buy styles that can be worn with ~~both pants and skirts~~ *various looks*. Ballet-inspired T-straps, espadrilles, strap sandals, classic pumps, high-heel moccasins, all *are versatile* ~~work just as well with either~~. And remember, there shouldn't be "summer" or "winter" shoes in a ~~Lifestyle~~ *Workable* Wardrobe—just "seasonless" shoes.

If you have to choose, always put your money in boots rather than shoes. They're more visible, they last longer and don't go out of style as quickly. In many climates, women are now wearing boots eight months out of the year.

HATS

There will always be hats. One way the executive woman can distinguish herself from the secretarial pool is to go to the office wearing a hat. Hats, more than any other ~~Addable~~ *accessory*, set a mood. For one thing, they're very obvious, even from a distance. A hat lends sophistication—it can be serious or amusing, it's not just for keeping your head warm.

When what you want is a little drama—even at work—a hat will never let you disappear into the woodwork. But it's got to look deliberate, not like an afterthought. It must pick up one of the colors in your outfit. If you're a hat person, put your money into several in the main colors of your ~~Lifestyle~~ Wardrobe. And if yours is a monochromatic wardrobe, so much the better. Hats are most effective as part of one-color dressing.

SCARVES

Scarves win the versatility contest hands down. But they can't, as you've been told, transform an outfit. That old trick only ends up looking like the same outfit with the addition of a scarf. The main role of scarves in a ~~Lifestyle~~ Wardrobe is to pick up the colors in your ~~Expandables~~, enabling each to be worn with the others. For example, if your ~~Continuous Color Scheme is~~ rust, beige, and cream, and you fall in love with a rust, cream, and teal blue scarf, buy it! You can now add some teal blue pieces to your wardrobe. The scarf will be the catalyst that holds it all together. Scarves work best when they're forging friendships between colors that usually clash.

A very well-dressed Milanese likes to throw a brilliant-colored silk scarf over the shoulder of her navy blue designer suit and white silk blouse. "Without it," she says laughingly, "I look like a stewardess on Alitalia."

Scarves come in a variety of sizes and shapes, and the larger the better. Size has impact. A shawl or oversize scarf can do more. It can double as a jacket and coverup; it can add a layer of warmth over a cape, coat, or suit. It looks marvelous thrown over the shoulder of your dress or jacket. It's practical enough for day wear and dramatic enough for evening wear.

A shawl-size scarf can do more than almost any other Addable. On Alice's trips to see the French and Italian collections, she always packs a shawl. She's come to depend on it as a catalyst for the colors in her travel wardrobe.

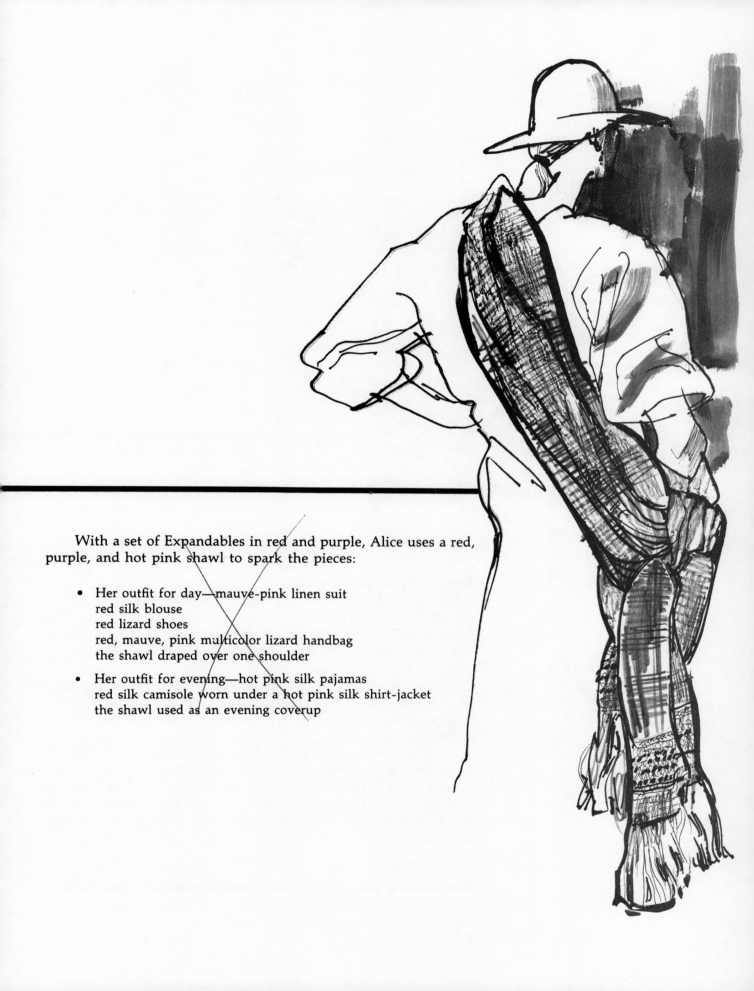

With a set of Expandables in red and purple, Alice uses a red, purple, and hot pink shawl to spark the pieces:

- Her outfit for day—mauve-pink linen suit
  red silk blouse
  red lizard shoes
  red, mauve, pink multicolor lizard handbag
  the shawl draped over one shoulder

- Her outfit for evening—hot pink silk pajamas
  red silk camisole worn under a hot pink silk shirt-jacket
  the shawl used as an evening coverup

To vary her look during the day, Alice can also pop the camisole under her linen suit jacket. The reason both day and evening combinations work so well for her is her shawl. Tossed over one shoulder, worn bandolier-style and knotted low, or used as a scarf, it always "makes a statement."

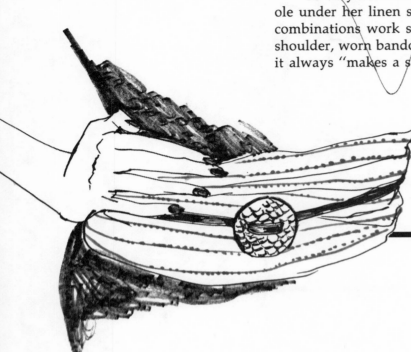

BELTS

A belt, ~~as you've seen~~, can be dynamite—the focal point of a whole look. A dark background sets the stage for a gold waist rope, a wide striped obi, a leather wrap with an Elsa Peretti buckle, a sash of some exotic fabric, a Navajo conch belt, or a Moroccan silver-tone girdle. The possibilities are endless.

The clothes strategy involved is called "Foreground Dressing." It works beautifully not only with belts, but with a pair of really fine boots, or a pair of "fantasy" shoes, or an unusual bag—or any of the Addables in this chapter.

There are some women, like DK, who choose to dress this way because their Addables are more interesting than anything else they own. It's also a way of simplifying their wardrobes. They're tipping the balance—with dramatic results—away from their clothes and toward a few precious objects that cry out for display, including important *jewelry*.

insert here from *Fashion Enuf* p16/19

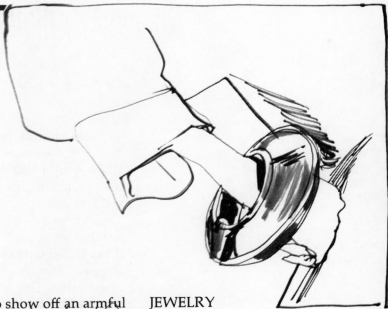

JEWELRY

F oreground Dressing is the best way to show off an armful of Bedouin bangles, an antique pendant, a gold neckwire. One dramatic piece of jewelry goes with almost anything —and gives everything more pizzazz.

The only danger here is having too much of a good thing. If you're featuring a large piece of jewelry, the effect is lost if you dilute it with other pieces of less consequence. We like the minimal approach when it comes to jewelry. Remember Chanel's dictum about simplicity? When you're dressed and ready to go, she'd say, take one last look in the mirror. Then strip off any piece of jewelry, any small interference that distracts from the *impact* of what you're wearing.

When it came to using jewelry in a witty, unexpected manner, there was no one to equal Chanel. Her "style" thrived on juxtaposition: The magnificent display of jewels on a simple little sweater-jacket became her trademark. So the rage for costume jewelry was born and some women, in their enthusiasm, loaded themselves like Christmas trees, thereby missing the point. Next time you're tempted by too much jewelry, remember Chanel.

You can take Addables one step further and use them to make any look uniquely your own. Here's where Addables really talk: When they appear over and over again to announce you . . . ("Of course I know DK, the woman with the marvelous belt"). This strategy is called "Trademark Dressing" and it's like "Foreground Dressing" in that it makes a strong visual impact. It also relies on repetition. The idea is to choose one Addable that says *you* to the world-at-large. It can be a certain kind of shoe, or a collection of caps, or a flower pinned to your lapel. It can even be a color. Once you choose it, never be without it.

We know a young woman who always wears gloves. She has an entire wardrobe of gloves from everyday white cotton to opulent elbow-length kid. What's memorable about her use of gloves is that it's so unusual these days. You think, "How nice that anyone would want to *bother.*"

A friend of Clara's wears her string of pearls everywhere: to the beach (but not into the water), to the ball, to the office. You can't think of her without them. "It's a good way to keep them healthy," she says, but that's not the real reason that she and her pearls are inseparable. She grew up with them. They're her trademark, and they look right with everything she owns.

Do you collect antique bar pins? Silk flowers? Lace handkerchiefs? Never be without them. Love shoes? Make yourself known for your cobalt suede "heels." Everyone should have the pleasure of her own trademark.

PUTTING ADDABLES TO WORK: MAKE A MANNEQUIN

Trying for a new look with old accessories? Mixing and matching for the first time, or for a special occasion? One of the toughest things to do is to put clothes and accessories together. Take a few extra minutes to play with your clothes a little—make a mannequin.

Put your outfit on the floor or bed and play the accessories against it. If you're planning on a scarf, put it at the neck. Wrap the belt you're sure is just right around the waist. Hosiery, shoes, or boots go below the hem, jewelry at the neck or exactly where you'd wear it.

Making a mannequin is a good way to develop your "eye." You'll find you can look at it and almost instantly see if something's missing, or something's got to go. And it's a lot easier to change a mannequin's clothes than your own.

By knowing beforehand exactly what you're going to put on, you'll avoid the last-minute frenzy—dashing from closet to drawer to shoe rack in order to put yourself together. Just borrow your mannequin's clothes.

THE RULE-BREAKERS

Break the "never wear white hose in the winter" rule by wearing white socks with gray flannel or black trousers and black patent leather pumps.

Forget the old adage about not "mixing good jewelry with junk" by twisting colored-stone necklaces with your real pearls or alternating dime-store enamel bracelets with your gold bangles.

Don't limit your metallic Addables to formal occasions.

The most effective Addables can be the least likely ones: an Indian spice box you use as an evening purse, a length of Mexican hand-embroidery you wrap as a belt.

Socialite Betsy Kaiser says, "The jewelry I love most are the pieces I can travel with. My kids gave me an Elsa Peretti 22-karat gold belt buckle that has ten interchangeable straps. The belt can be worn in suede, leather, or satin, depending on how dressed up I am, and I wear it everywhere. . . ."

Designer Mary McFadden: "My favorite jewel is my Verdura watch that I bought when I was seventeen years old."

Carolina Herrera wears a diamond bow with all her evening clothes, either in her hair or pinned to a black velvet ribbon around her wrist.

Sylvia de Waldner's trademark piece is, quite simply, her engagement ring mounted with two small pansy flowers.

The Paris editor of a famous American fashion magazine recently bought a pair of large, kite-shaped gold earrings and "hasn't taken them off since." They look marvelous with her dressy clothes but work just as well with her man-tailored daytime pantsuits. "It's probably their 'shock' value," she says, but it's impossible to think of her now without thinking of those earrings.

Who can forget Bella Abzug's hats? Gloria Steinem's aviator glasses? Louise Nevelson's spiky eyelashes, headscarf, and gold space shoes? Dolly Parton's wigs? Jacqueline Kennedy Onassis in pillbox hats when she was first lady and in outsized sunglasses today?

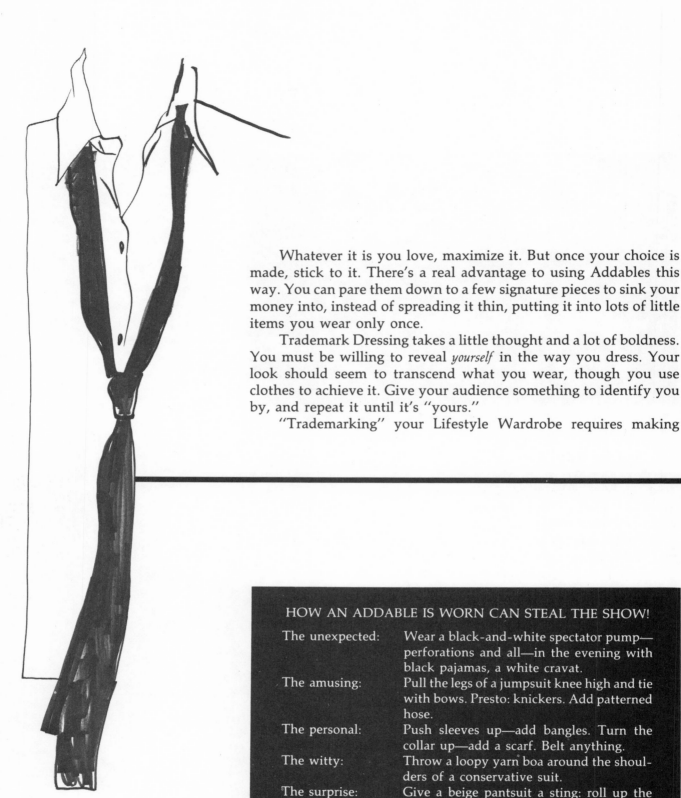

Whatever it is you love, maximize it. But once your choice is made, stick to it. There's a real advantage to using Addables this way. You can pare them down to a few signature pieces to sink your money into, instead of spreading it thin, putting it into lots of little items you wear only once.

Trademark Dressing takes a little thought and a lot of boldness. You must be willing to reveal *yourself* in the way you dress. Your look should seem to transcend what you wear, though you use clothes to achieve it. Give your audience something to identify you by, and repeat it until it's "yours."

"Trademarking" your Lifestyle Wardrobe requires making

HOW AN ADDABLE IS WORN CAN STEAL THE SHOW!

The unexpected:	Wear a black-and-white spectator pump—perforations and all—in the evening with black pajamas, a white cravat.
The amusing:	Pull the legs of a jumpsuit knee high and tie with bows. Presto: knickers. Add patterned hose.
The personal:	Push sleeves up—add bangles. Turn the collar up—add a scarf. Belt anything.
The witty:	Throw a loopy yarn boa around the shoulders of a conservative suit.
The surprise:	Give a beige pantsuit a sting: roll up the pants a touch, to show hot pink socks.

SIGNATURE ACCESSORIES FOR SUITS

Lace jabot
Man's bow tie
Silk scarf tied in a bow
Stock tie
Bare neck and a necklace
Fur piece, gloves, and a little veiled hat
Velvet string tie
Fur or yarn boa
Pocket handkerchief
Flower on lapel
Lapel pin, stickpin, antique lapel watch

choices, but the reward is a personal style that singles you out from the crowd. Addables practically do it for you—they can be among the most individual items you'll ever own. It goes back to the whole point about Addables in general: They're Expandables with an infinite vocabulary. Learn to use them so they speak your language. A bronze strap evening sandal can look smashing on a summer day with something as tailored as a white pinstripe linen suit. A Lurex glitter scarf gives a jolt of surprise when tucked into a tailored outfit. It's the juxtaposition of flash against something conservative that gives the look its wit. Many evening Addables can lead two lives —day and night.

11. Spotting the Fashion Trends

Many women feel that fashion is "the Enemy."
At the beginning of each new season it seems that a whole new look is being sprung at you: Mini, Midi, Maxi, padded shoulders, natural shoulders, blouson, sheath, big-look, dolman, skimp—and all when you're not looking. Afraid that your costly purchases will end up as cast-offs the following season, you buy "safe" or you don't buy at all.

Fashion is often considered a conspiracy calculated to make us look ridiculous—and become poorer—by a coterie of designers who are "out to get us." We've all heard, "They'll never force *me* into those longer / shorter / fuller / tighter skirts." But who's repeating that refrain? It's the woman who doesn't know how to spot the fashion trends—the one who invariably buys last year's style this year and wonders why she never gets her money's worth, the one who carries on a running battle with fashion—who *always* loses.

However fickle it may seem, fashion doesn't come to a sudden halt each season and reverse gears only to take off in another direction. *FASHION CHANGES ARE PREDICTABLE.* When you become aware of the basic elements that reflect fashion's changes, you'll always have time to adapt your wardrobe without traumatic shocks to your budget.

Fashion changes are never revolutionary—always evolutionary. There is a predictable transition in silhouette, rather than a sharp transformation. Most style changes are a long time coming in and a long time going out.

Basic fashion trends are always concerned with *proportion.* Changing hem lengths are only the most noticeable—and the easiest to adjust by yourself. There are other equally important factors:

- the width of the shoulder—natural or exaggerated—and armhole fit

- The placement of the waistline—high, low, or natural

- Shape—flared, straight, voluminous, body-hugging

These proportions add up to a mood: elegant and formal in the 1950s, radical in the 1960s, casual in the 1970s, eclectic in the 1980s. That's why shortening a ten-year-old dress doesn't put it back in style. Chances are that the other proportions are out of fashion too and will clash with the current mood of fashion. In other words, styles never come back in the same way.

You don't have to be a dedicated clothes horse to *follow the trends.* Read the early spring and late summer issues of *Vogue* and *Harper's Bazaar* (watch for the covers that indicate that the next season's fashions are being featured). Read the semiannual fashion supplement of your newspaper and the department store catalogs.

When you read these publications, don't just look at the photos. *Read* the editorials that discuss the fashions. The editorial pages will give you the scoop. The illustrations won't give you the message unless you read the captions. The clues to a major style change are phrases like:

- "Watch for . . ."

- "What you'll be seeing"
- "New signals"
- "Coming up"
- "What's needed now"
- "Keep your eye on . . ."
- "The BIG news is . . ."

Window shopping can be as instructive about upcoming trends as reading fashion magazines and catalogs. What you see in them will give you an idea about:

- the newest shapes and proportions
- how colors and textures are used in combinations
- pant and skirt lengths
- the shoes that work best with skirts, pants, and dresses and the stocking colors and textures to wear with them
- how accessories are used

As soon as you begin to read about or see a completely new look, not just a yearly or seasonal update of the current look, you can be certain that this means business. A new look is on the way!

If a new style or silhouette seems imminent, declare a halt on buying. Purchases you make at this transitional time may prove wrong. You may be buying the old style—the one that's on the way out—and wasting your precious clothing dollars. It can happen even to those women who have loads of fashion savvy.

So, stop buying! Get by on what you already have in your wardrobe. This is the time to save your money—you'll need it when the new style becomes current fashion. Once the new style is "in" you can do some heavy purchasing. A style lasts for a few years and you'll have that entire length of time to wear your purchases.

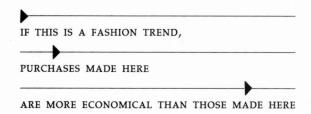

IF THIS IS A FASHION TREND,

PURCHASES MADE HERE

ARE MORE ECONOMICAL THAN THOSE MADE HERE

If Ann K., a top-level executive, had been paying closer attention to the fashion press in 1969, she would never have bought the mini-length Geoffrey Beene coat-and-dress ensemble that she fell in love with during one spring lunch hour. Too busy to have the slight alterations made right away, Ann hung it in her closet until fall, when she was looking forward to wearing it.

Little did she expect that this would be the fall that the Mini fell to midi-length. There was no way to wear the Beene ensemble without looking ridiculous. There was no way to alter the hemline. Ann had lost her investment and missed wearing an outfit she loved.

But she learned an expensive lesson: Don't put money into a style at the end of its life cycle!

The key to getting the most out of your fashion dollars is knowing as much as possible as soon as possible.

B ut what are fads? A fad can be almost anything:

- A fad can be a *color*—fuchsia, teal.

- A fad can be an *accessory*—platform shoes, hair picks, feather pins.

- A fad can be a *piece of clothing*—nailhead-studded jeans, T-shirts with messages.

- A fad can be a *look*—Annie Hall, Military, Punk-Rocker.

It's a short-lived flight of fancy; it's disposable fashion.

Should you completely ignore fads? No. They're fun and amusing, they're cheap and—yes, useful. Useful, for they can update your Lifestyle Wardrobe. And fads can connect you to the present. If you ignore them you risk looking matronly. *Vogue* says, "Don't forget that fad has a place in fashion. It has wit and it gives pleasure."

Fads, even more than "serious fashion," tend to mark an era. Fashion sets the general style; Think of the football shoulders of the 1940s, the dirndl skirts of the 1950s. But it's the details one always remembers best: the snoods and silly tipped hats of the 1940s; the

YOU CAN'T TALK ABOUT *FASHION* WITHOUT TALKING ABOUT *FADS*.

black leotard beatnik look of the 1950s that Juliette Greco popularized in the boîtes of St. Germain-des-Près. In the 1960s, fashion was Sassoon's "wedge" haircut, the white Courrèges boots, and Mary Quant's little-girl look. By the 1970s the fads were hot pants and gun belts. They stood out against yards of boring blue jeans and tie-dyed T-shirts.

How does a fad happen? Why is it that one day every store in America is stocking automobile-mechanic suits or poor-boy sweaters? There can be many reasons, not the least of which is that the eye gets used to clothes very fast. We tend to tire of "the same old thing" with increasing rapidity. We crave change.

Change is what fashion is all about. But it takes time to introduce a whole new trend. Long-term trends are based on changes in proportion that require a whole shift of gears. Meanwhile, we can have the newness we crave in little, less expensive ways. That's where fads come in.

But fads respond to a general fashion climate, too. They don't come out of a vacuum. When did we last see the "preppy" look of recent vintage? In the 1950s at college. And the 1950s were a time of relative stability, of conformity and economic optimism. Thirty years later, in more troubled times, we look back at that period and want what it gave us then. Sooner than you can snap your fingers, the cutting tables are full of button-down oxford cloth shirts, shirtdresses, chino pants, polo shirts. It's not a major style change; it's a fad.

A fad can also come about as a reaction to fashion trends the public just won't swallow. Were hot pants a reaction to the midi? We've all been retroed back through the 1920s, 1930s, 1940s, 1950s and even the 1960s. Designers can't go backward any longer, nor can they seem to go forward. They can't even steal from abroad any longer, since Paris and Milan have gone their own way with oddities like tough leather jumpsuits, plastic breastplates and even, in one recent collection,—hobbleskirts. Hobbleskirts!

Fads follow a standard life cycle. Once American manufacturers launched the "preppy" look, every department and specialty store in the country carried "preppy" clothes. There was a run on pink oxford cloth and the original maker of classic moccasins in Maine could hardly keep stores stocked with its penny loafers. Green and pink were the colors of the season. Cotton turtlenecks printed with turtles and whales appeared everywhere.

Like everything that becomes successful, soon there were knock-offs—copies of the fad. There was bargain-basement preppy, sportswear preppy, high-priced preppy. You could have your preppy any way you wanted it, at any price range.

But after a season or two, a fad like this reaches a saturation point. We're all sick of green and pink, of little turtles and crocodiles. We need some new treat for the eye. And so "preppy" fades and disappears, and something unexpected and fresh takes its place. Meanwhile, we've all had the chance to add another dimension to the way we've been dressing: perhaps a pair of those dependable loafers or some bright polo shirts to wear with the pants we already own. An addition can be as small as a headband or as witty as wearing a string of pearls with a camp-shirt and shorts. Whatever it may have been, "preppy" provided a certain diversion at the moment and gave us a range of options for new ways of focusing our own look. It was fun. And that, after all, is exactly what a fad is for.

Like other kinds of clothing, a fad can be thought of as a tool. Its strength is in its *specificity.* Since it has the power to summon up the style of a whole period in our lives, it becomes a potent force,

CHOOSE SOME CLOTHES THAT ARE OUT OF FASHION

Who is the woman who always appears dressed in the very "latest"? Was she born yesterday? What did she wear last year? Is she so extravagant that she never wears her clothes two years in a row or so charitable that she literally gives people the "clothes off her back"? Somehow it makes you suspicious that she never owned anything good enough to hold onto.

The late Gloria Guinness, considered by many the world's most elegant woman, said that she never wore clothes that were obviously "new." "All new" is never the answer for a well-dressed look. If you follow the Lifestyle Wardrobe strategies, you'll know what to hang onto from past seasons and how to update it with the fashions and fads you'll buy. In that way you'll give yourself a clothes past as well as a fashion future.

and you'll want to learn how to use it effectively. Used well, a fad item can sharpen up everything you wear.

So be aware of fads. Learn to "scan" popular trends in the streets, in the magazines, in the store windows. Take from them what suits *your* needs. By all means buy the fad of the moment right away if it fits your frame of mind and your Lifestyle Wardrobe.

During a morning rush hour Clara noticed a young woman poised, briefcase in hand, waiting for the light to change. She was expensively dressed in a cream-colored, nubby-textured wool suit over a cream silk blouse. Her shoes and handbag were good brown leather. She looked polished and very much on the way up. But something puzzled Clara. Why did this woman look so boring when everything she had on was so attractive? As the light changed and the woman started across the street, it came in a flash: What she needed was the touch of the fad of that moment—a feather pin—

on her lapel. That current "rage" would have added the visual spark to bring her whole look into focus. It would have animated her outfit the way a smile lights a face. And it would have placed her suit solidly in the current season.

Precisely because fads have such a strong power to recall a particular time, they must be worn intensively and then discarded —*promptly.* A good rule of thumb is to stop wearing yours just as soon as everyone else abandons theirs. What could be more depressing than seeing a woman today in nailhead-studded jeans? Or a military hip belt? Or the fatigue hat of the late 1970s?

Some fads do keep showing up: textured hose, the Safari look, the Western fringed jacket, American Indian jewelry, patchwork, the jeans skirt. "Ethnic" fads are hardy perennials, and are, in effect, Eclectic Classics.

But by and large, a fad's just one of the delightful small ways in which you "connect" with what's around you by the way you dress. To take it too seriously would be to miss the point. But to miss out on fads altogether would be a shame.

During their short life, fads are copied at all price levels. The most expensive stores are usually first with current fads but by the time you're aware of them, the medium-price stores are selling them, and very quickly those on the bottom of the price scale have them, too. Of all the various versions of fad items, there is often no difference in look and not too much difference in quality. Since they aren't designed to last it pays to buy the medium- or even the lower-priced fad items.

Knowing how to spot the trends will give you the self-assurance to buy the most expensive fashion you can afford. It will also give you the confidence to incorporate some fads into your wardrobe—at the least expensive price. If fashion trends give you the look of this season, fads give you the look of this minute.

12. Savvy Shopping

T o dress well you must know how to shop. Your Lifestyle Chart will act as your shopping guide. The chart tells you how you spend your time, so you can be more realistic than most women are about what clothes you need. You know your basic colors. You've learned how to build a Lifestyle Wardrobe from component parts. You know how to work with Addables. And you've learned how to tell a fashion trend from a fad.

Now you're going to learn how to shop like a professional. A savvy shopper knows *where* to buy, *when* to buy, and *how* to buy. Does the idea of shopping fill you with dread? Most women, at one time or another, have felt overwhelmed by the choice of merchandise, by aggressive saleshelp—or by no saleshelp at all. The reaction can range from a migraine headache to sheer panic. What's worse, "shoppingphobia" inevitably produces a thrown-together look—the result of random selections made in desperation.

Shoppingphobia is easier to conquer than you might think. The trick is preselection. Many stores help you with a "street of shops" or boutiques, but no store can possibly narrow down the choices enough to meet your particular needs. You have to do it yourself.

The technique: *zeroing in.* It works like speed reading—you take in many different kinds of information all at once. You're looking for a particular item, of a particular color, size, and price. It may be color that strikes you first. When you see *your* color, zero in. If the Expandable you're looking for isn't there in your color, move on fast. Don't try on anything that doesn't stand a chance. You'll only deplete your energy and your time on a loser.

Zeroing in takes the pain out of shopping. When you get the hang of it you'll find yourself checking out your favorite shopping haunts more frequently but using the fitting room less often. The more you know about what's available, the less effort you waste. In the end, it's *frequent* shopping which saves you time.

A savvy shopper knows **where** to buy. To begin with there are *department stores.* Their size and complexity means that they offer the largest selection and the most services:

DEPARTMENT STORES

- telephone and mail order

- regular and installment charge accounts

- catalogs

- gift wrapping

- alterations

- delivery service

- easy return and exchange procedures

- personal shopping service

- expanded shopping hours

- convenient snack bars, restrooms, and telephones

- freedom to browse

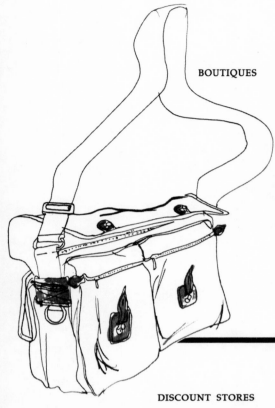

BOUTIQUES

Next come the *boutiques.* There are two kinds: first, the specialty store chains found on shopping streets and in malls throughout the country. Their selections and price ranges are well defined and geared to a particular lifestyle—juniors, young career, active sports, and so forth. The second kind is the individually owned shop. While such a shop has less of a selection, it's quicker and easier to discover if it has what you're looking for. It's also more likely that you can find a salesperson there who will give you individual attention, alerting you to special merchandise and special sales, understanding your needs and helping you make your selection.

If you can find a boutique that carries the kind of merchandise that fits your lifestyle—your look and your price—there's no better way to shop. The merchandise has been preselected for you and it's easier to spot the trends here.

DISCOUNT STORES

Discount stores may seem anything but chic places to shop, but by zeroing in you can buy things here you couldn't afford at department-store or boutique prices. There are two types of discounters: the large discount chains and the smaller discount boutiques. The large chains often have good values, but, for the most part, you get what you pay for.

The discount boutiques that sell designer clothes off-price are an excellent source for good buys, provided you know what's current. The trick is to shop the better stores before you shop the discount boutiques. That way you won't end up with last year's closeout or this year's dog. You'll recognize the merchandise that's currently selling for more elsewhere.

OTHER SHOPPING OPTIONS

There are other shopping possibilities you may not have considered:

- If you have a small frame, check out the *boys' departments* for blazers, shirts, jeans and trousers, and sweaters. Boys' sweaters, for example, are much more reasonably priced than women's sweaters of the same quality and often better looking. Many women who want

Ralph Lauren's styling without Ralph Lauren's prices buy the boys' Polo line.

- *Sporting goods stores* are an excellent place to find heavy sweaters, rugged sportswear and outerwear, and rainwear. There are wonderful (and less expensive) blazers, shirts and ascots, and boots at stores that specialize in outfitting horseback riders. You can also put together a great Western outfit in these stores, and don't overlook their large selection of authentic jeans.

  Sporting goods stores are great places to find some intriguing possibilities for handbags. Their items are constructed to take lots of wear and tear and the prices are lower than you'll find in most handbag departments. Look for:

  —Canvas fishing bags that make great shoulder pouches
  —Suede cartridge bags that look wonderful with casual sportswear
  —Wicker fishing baskets to wear with summer sportswear
  —Water-repellent nylon bags to tote books, leotards, and business papers

- *Lingerie departments and shops* are an excellent source for evening wear, swimwear, and active sportswear. All the name designers are now producing sleepwear and loungewear and many of these gowns and pajamas and robes could be worn for parties and formal occasions. And they'll cost you far less than a similar gown or pajamas from the same designer's regular collections.

Loungewear made of terry cloth or sweat-shirt fabric doubles as active sportswear or beachwear, and Lycra body suits and leotards make the best, and the least expensive, swimsuits you can buy.

- *Notions departments and shops* are the best places to find ribbons for belts and scarves. Look for the latest fad items: feather pins, flowers, lace collars, beaded collrs in *trimmings stores.* You'll find ropes and tassels for belts in *upholstery shops.*

- *Linen shops and departments* sell small blankets and throws you can use as ponchos and shawls.

- *Oriental shops* are a good source for quilted silk or cotton jackets and flat black Mary Jane shoes.

- *Indian boutiques* offer goods which, in the store itself, may overdazzle —even look cheap—but in your own setting, away from an overabundance of color and embroidery, can look special and expensive. These shops are excellent places to find unique summer and evening wear.

- *Five-and-tens* are great places to shop! You can find inexpensive beach sandals, cowboy bandannas, straw hats, beach bags, bangle bracelets, socks, and stockings. The woolen berets sold there are the same quality as those sold in department stores at three times the price.

- *Dance stores* are another source for swimsuits, and the ballet and dance shoes that look so good with summer clothes.

- *Mail-order shopping* is increasingly popular as women find themselves with less time to shop. Many find it easier to choose what they want from a small, seemingly personal booklet than in a large, impersonal store. Over $30 billion in sales are done by mail order each year.

  Size could be a problem here. But all reputable mail-order houses make exchanges and refunds and, once you're sure of the fit and size breakdown in your favorite catalog, you can order *anything* without hesitation. Remember: Apparel in the size range Petite-Small-Medium-Large requires a less precise fit than apparel in numbered sizes (8/9, 10/11, etc.). Look for it when you order by mail.

  The large chains and department and specialty stores and hundreds of smaller mail-order houses all put out catalogs that feature a wide variety of first-quality merchandise. And orders are filled promptly—usually within 30 days.

A savvy shopper knows **when** to buy. For regular-price merchandise the best time is in advance of the season when the stores' selection peaks—August for fall/winter and March for spring/summer. Remember, there are really only two seasons for the customer. Four seasons remain for the retailer a means of increasing sales and turning over stock. Winter clothes work just as well in the fall and early spring and summer clothes can also be worn in the late spring and early fall. And as more and more of your Lifestyle Wardrobe becomes seasonless you'll think less and less about winter versus summer clothes.

Nearly every item of clothing goes on sale sometime during the year. These sales usually run on a regular schedule—when stores clear out their inventory or prepare to receive new stock. Some of your clothing purchases can be timed to take advantage of the savings. But size, style, and color selections may be inadequate, so the things you buy on sale should be the extra purchases—not your investment clothes.

To shop the sales like an expert: pick your favorite store, or, narrowing your hunting grounds even further, your favorite department in your favorite store. Early in the season study the merchandise; even try on the likely candidates. Then wait for the end-of-season clearance. Learn the regular prices so you can tell which merchandise is really a bargain. Watch and wait. You could get lucky!

But don't buy an item just because it's been reduced. Be sure that whatever you buy on sale meets your usual standards of quality and taste. And be sure it's still in style. Many women make the mistake of buying something on sale that's *on* sale precisely because it's no longer in style. A real bargain is something that fits into your Lifestyle Wardrobe, or it's no bargain at all. It isn't calculated in dollars but in wearability. A "bargain" that spends the season in your closet is a bad buy!

A calendar of sales events may help you plan your "buys."

The retailer's terminology will tell you if you're really getting a bargain:

CLEARANCE SALE: Regular merchandise marked down because it's late in the season.

SPECIAL PURCHASE: Merchandise brought into the store especially for a sale—could be of a quality inferior to that which the store usually carries.

COMPARABLE VALUE: Merchandise is similar but not identical to higher-priced merchandise.

LIQUIDATION SALE:	Store is going out of business and needs to dispose of the stock.
AS-IS:	Regular merchandise that has been damaged.
IRREGULAR:	Merchandise has a slight defect.
SECOND:	Merchandise may have an obvious defect.

A savvy shopper knows **how** to buy. Here are some of the tricks of the trade:

COLOR CARDS   You can't carry color in your head. If you want to match something, cut off a small piece of fabric from an inside seam and staple it onto an index card. You can carry the card in your handbag—it's smaller and easier to tote around than the item itself.

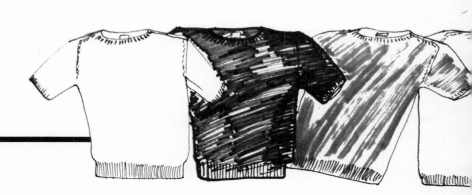

BUYING IN MULTIPLES   There are four good reasons for buying the same article in several colors or fabrics:

1. It's a time-saver. If an item works well for you, why look for something else? Each Sunday the magazine sections of the newspapers carry full-color ads for sweaters, blouses, dresses, and accessories in a wide range of colors. Notice how different the same item looks in a dark color, a neutral, or a bright.

2. It's a money saver if the item is on sale.

3. It gives you style continuity. Having a turtleneck sweater or a bow blouse in several colors helps to establish your "look."

4. If size is your problem and you find an item that fits, stock up. Mallory Hathaway, partner in Hathaway de La Chapelle, a New York public relations firm, is tall. Finding pants that fit well is a problem. When she dicovers a pair that fits and looks great on her, she buys several in different colors.

Certain items are naturals for buying this way:

BUYING IN MULTIPLES
FOR COLOR VARIETY

Berets Five-and-ten-cent store variety, affordable in every color of the rainbow.

Eyeglass frames Choose the dominant colors of your Lifestyle Wardrobe. Make sure you stick to the same shape. It will give you a consistent look and, at the same time, allow you to switch lenses from reading to sunglasses to suit your mood.

Watch straps Slide in a new one when your color mood changes.

Socks Most people don't focus on them. *Vogue* fashion editor Polly Mellon does: They're her favorite clothes variable. "I love socks. I use them as a surprise a lot. Warm brown, pale blue ribbed, pale yellow, terra-cotta, anything with a little glitter for night, Argyles. I love the look of a pattern coming out of your pants."

There are two types of impulse buys: good (those we're glad we made) and bad (those we regret later on). You can learn to distinguish between the two by using a mental checklist. Ask yourself: Why am I buying this unplanned item? Because it's on sale? To chase the blues? Because someone else is buying it? I can't live without it, it's "me"?

CREATIVE IMPULSE BUYING

If you can't live without it and it really is "you," is it compatible with your Lifestyle Wardrobe? Does it fit into your Continuous Color Concept? If it doesn't, is it worth buying companion items for? If the item will complement your Lifestyle Wardrobe, buy it if

97

you can. It will give you pleasure and, most likely, lots of wearings.

But if you're attracted to the item only because it's on sale, because someone else (maybe a friend) is buying it, or to chase the blues, leave the store immediately. Make a cheaper, substitute purchase like a lipstick, if you *must* buy something. And congratulate yourself on having avoided a mistake in your closet.

CHASING THE BLUES

Spending a little mad money on something frivolous is an excellent safety valve. Inexpensive pleasures—cosmetics, textured pantyhose, a leotard, sunglasses, and lapel flowers are a guilt-free way to give yourself a lift. Blues chasers are the small purchases that make you feel like a million.

DESIGNER LABELS—
TO HAVE OR HAVE NOT

Designer labels have been sweeping the country since the late 1960s. But the designer-as-status-giver dates back to fourteenth-century Florence where the leather guilds demanded that each craftsman do his work in the presence of judges and then "sign" his creation—thereby initiating signature leather goods. In the 1880s in France a pair of initials began to appear on the expensive suitcases of a luggage maker whose name was Louis Vuitton. The fact that Vuitton travel cases sold for astronomical sums meant that they were automatically status symbols: The LV initials they bore were mere confirmation of their value.

Gucci, Hermès and other quality European manufacturers followed suit in what was to become an elite circle of luxury goods all of which bore the discreet initials of their designer. Meanwhile, the American economy boomed and consumers on this side of the Atlantic coveted these expensive symbols of affluence.

But, whereas in the past the signature item came from the designer's own atelier, ailing couture industries on both sides of the Atlantic had found a new way to bolster their empires: licensing. In no time at all, designers were allowing perfume, accessories, and popular-priced versions of their couture designs to be mass-marketed. Within the next decade we had CD, YSL, BB, and DVF on everything from chocolates to sunglasses; from bathtowels to wine. King of the licensor is still Pierre Cardin, who does $50 million annually in licensing royalties. The status landslide was well under way.

Next came designer jeans in the 1970s. Gloria Vanderbilt, Calvin Klein, Ralph Lauren, Liz Claiborne, all signed their jeans; the sales volumes were staggering. The trend continues. Over $250 million worth of merchandise annually still sells under the Sasson label, for example. The designers themselves became superstars.

Are designer labels on clothes a good investment? Are they worth the extra money you pay for them? And exactly what are you paying for? It depends on your point of view and on your lifestyle.

CLARA: "I don't buy designer labels. I figure you're paying for a security blanket and who needs that? When it comes to a psychological boost I prefer ice cream. Another problem is that knock-offs and copies ruin a designer look—if it's successful in the first place —once it appears. I like to zero in on designer clothes for ideas, but as a free-lance writer I have the time and flexibility to save money by buying look-alikes or putting together my own "designer" outfits in less expensive versions.

"Then, I have to admit that so much of my time is spent writing that I don't need to look up-to-the-mark every minute. When I *do* go out to meet with an editor I have some very well-thought-out ensembles to choose from—and that's it."

ALICE: "I buy designer clothes because they give me another tool to work with. I know exactly where I'm heading in my career and also know that my clients and colleagues recognize and respond to a

YOU CAN'T ALWAYS FIGURE THE FIT

Most women feel that if something doesn't fit perfectly right off the rack, there's something wrong.

Remind yourself of the way men buy their clothes: They have them altered without a thought and always get a perfect fit.

There's nothing wrong with having alterations done on garments that are really *worth* altering.

TRYING IT ON FOR SIZE

If you like something, take it into the fitting room in two or three sizes. There's no such thing as standardized sizing and your usual 8 may fit like a 6 or a 10.

By taking the next larger and smaller sizes into the fitting room you'll eliminate the need to get dressed in order to search for another garment or to try to snare a salesperson's attention from behind the dressing-room door.

GOOD TIMING HELPS

Know the best times to shop:

Monday, Tuesday, and Friday are the least crowded days, and Wednesday, Thursday, and Saturday the most crowded.

Stores are emptiest in the early morning, midafternoon, and evening. Lunchtime and late afternoon are very busy.

Remember that stores are always less crowded when the weather is bad. A rainy day is the best time to have your favorite store all to yourself.

high-fashion look. It would be cutting off my nose to spite my face *not* to wear designer clothes.

"Then there's another point: I estimate that designer garments give me about three years of concentrated wear. I get an 'advance' look at the top of the season in which I buy them, plus two extra years of wear before the look turns 'old.' The designers I buy from are far ahead of fashion and I profit from their advanced styling. For my kind of work, designer labels actually represent a net *gain.* And my time is so limited, I can't afford to spend it trying to put together my own looks. I let the designers do it for me. They're my greatest time-savers."

DIANE S., head of her own public relations firm, believes so strongly in designer clothes that she has a representative from Halston come to her office at the beginning of each season. Together they decide which pieces to add to her growing collection of that designer's clothes and which, if any, to discard. Diane has never looked better and, she adds, "My business is terrific!"

American design has come into its own. Seventh Avenue has become the world center for creative ready-to-wear and has given us a host of designer names to reckon with:

- GEOFFREY BEENE: a fine hand for tailoring. Exquisite European styling and detail.

- BILL BLASS: clothes that have great poise and presence. A simple, composed, timeless quality.

- STEPHEN BURROWS: bright, sexy clothes in electric colors. Invented the ruffle-edged "lettuce hem."

- PERRY ELLIS: young, witty sportswear. Invented the "dimple" sleeve.

- HALSTON: American minimalism at its best, zipperless, buttonless elegance. Notable for his one-shoulder dress.

- CAROL HORN: An "idiomatic" designer, right in the American grain. Loves layering.

- ANNE KLEIN: classic American sportswear of great elegance.

- CALVIN KLEIN: casual chic in sophisticated color combinations and rich fabrics.

- RALPH LAUREN: a traditionalist whose range goes from English-tweedy to American-Indian to his famed "Gatsby" look.

- MARY MCFADDEN: mannered, "artistic" clothes. Known for her Fortuny-like crystal pleating.

- OSCAR DE LA RENTA: the look of opulence in daytime and evening clothes.

- GIORGIO DI ST. ANGELO: known for clever, ethnic clothes, but equally inventive with bodywear.

- ZORAN: the essence of modern, artful dressing, little interference of detail.

IT PAYS TO COMPARE

When shopping for a handbag, comparing leather with plastic will show you how to recognize the good texture of leather at a glance. Look for double stitching and riveted buckles and small studs at the bottom of the bag—they mean extra durability. Shoulder straps or handles should have a ½-inch or more seam allowance so they won't pull loose. Inside pockets should be as deep as the bag itself. That way you'll avoid an unsightly center bulge.

If you're buying pants, zero in on the fabric. Loose weaves may cause the pants to lose their shape; heavy tweeds can look bulky. Your best choice is a medium-weight tighter weave. If you buy pants with a lining, make sure the lining is tacked to the hem. And hem, seams, zippers, and pockets should all lie flat without puckering.

TOPS FIRST

When trying on a two-piece dress, suit, or pantsuit, always try the top on first. Don't bother with the bottom until you're sure the top—the most important piece—fits and is becoming.

BEST BITS

When you're shopping, think of the many ways to use scarves. Or keep an open mind about using other items in place of scarves.

- Look for men's silk pocket handkerchiefs to wear in *your* blazer pocket.

- Look for pretty table napkins large enough to roll or fold into neckerchiefs.

- Look for silky bow ties that can be worn at the collar of a tailored shirt by day and—a witty touch—as a choker above a strapless evening top.

- Look for a man's striped tie wide enough to be wound around your waist as a belt. Or use two in complementary or contrasting colors as a cummerbund.

Stores today are entertainment. They offer ingenious displays, dramatic decor, a place to see and be seen. Shopping is a form of theater with you as part of the cast. It's meant to be enjoyed, not feared.

13. Closet Smarts

Closet smarts are simple. The point to remember is: *The purpose of a closet isn't storage—it's display.*

Your closet should be thought of as a showcase for your Lifestyle Wardrobe. If it's well organized, it enhances your use of your clothes, showing off the whole range of put-togethers you've been building up based on the Lifestyle Wardrobe method.

If, on the other hand, you pack things away, neat but unseen, you'll be defeating the whole idea behind the Lifestyle Wardrobe, which is to create as many outfits as possible with the fewest number of Expandables. Here's how to get it all out in the open:

Organize your closet by lifestyle categories, giving the most easily accessible space to the clothes you spend most of your time in. It works exactly like your Lifestyle Wardrobe chart. If most of your chart is red, your clothes for work should be given the most space. Within the "work" category, hang each piece according to classification: pants, skirts, shirts and blouses, jackets, dresses. Do not hang suits together; separate skirts from their jackets. That way you'll *wear* them as separates.

Next take your second-largest color block on the chart and hang that category in the same way. Continue through all the categories on your chart, giving each one its own space. That way you'll spot the "crossover" possibilities from one category to the next as well as have what you need for each activity well organized and at hand.

And why not color-key your hangers to correspond to the colors on your Lifestyle Chart? Department stores, drugstores, variety stores, even supermarkets, all carry plastic hangers in enough colors for you to match the categories of clothes in your wardrobe.

In organizing your closet:

- Never hang one garment over another—each must be separately visible to make the system work.

- Never hang by outfit—the pieces "lock in" to each other and it will be harder to separate them visually.

- Never organize according to frequency of use—it's the best way to forget what you own. Everything you have for current wear should be on view, even if you have to convert a bookcase for the purpose or put a free-standing clothes rack behind a screen.

- Never hang fur, suede, or angora near velvet, wool, corduroy, or any fabric that traps shedding.

When you've completed your closet organization, **Make a ClothesWise Chart for your closet door.**

Here's where you get to see your accomplishment in writing. The ClothesWise Chart lists all the clothing possibilities you've built up with your Expandables and Addables. The chart can be erased, added to, and changed as you add and subtract from your Lifestyle Wardrobe. It's your dailydressing computer.

CLOTHESWISE CHART

▨	Work *(green)*
▨	Dress-up *(purple)*
▨	Exercise/Active Sports *(red)*
▤	Casual Home *(yellow)*
▦	Casual Out *(blue)*

Expandables	Addables
Red suit/white blouse	Large black handbag/Narrow black belt/Black pumps
Red jacket/black pants/print dress top	Large black handbag/Wide red belt/Black pumps
Print dress skirt/black turtleneck/red jacket	Large black handbag Red sandals
Red skirt/black turtleneck	Paisley shawl/Large black handbag/Red sandals
2-piece dress under black jacket	Red clutch bag Black pumps
Black pants suit/black camisole	Red belt/Red clutch bag/Red sandals
2-piece dress, top open over black camisole	Red clutch bag Red sandals
Black pants/white blouse	Paisley shawl/Red clutch bag/Red belt/Red sandals
Red jacket/black pants/lumberjack shirt	Large black handbag/Narrow black belt/Black pumps
Black pants/black turtleneck/lumberjack shirt worn as jacket	Red clutch bag/Red belt worn over jacket/Black pumps
Black pants/print dress worn as overblouse	Red sandals
Black pants/black turtleneck	Paisley shawl worn as obi sash/Red sandals

CLOTHESWISE CHART

▨ Work (green)

▨ Dress-up (purple)

▨ Exercise/Active Sports (red)

▨ Casual Home (yellow)

▨ Casual Out (blue)

Expandables	Addables

You'll see how much easier it is to get dressed every morning when a glance at the chart on your closet door tells you exactly what Expandables and Addables to pull out. Your only job from now on is to keep the "filing system" in order by updating the chart and by keeping your clothes "on-the-ready" with repairs when needed.

As with your Lifestyle Chart and your closet hangers, each item listed in the ClothesWise Chart can be written in the color corresponding to its lifestyle category.

The variety of closet hardware can be bewildering unless you keep one cardinal rule in mind: Look for what will make your clothes *visible.* Avoid storage containers such as those matched garment bags, shoe files, and hatboxes (usually in quilted plastic or fabric) that don't let you see what's inside. Garment bags *are* a good idea for very fragile evening clothes and for all out-of-season garments. Just make sure that any closet accessory you buy is either see-through vinyl or windowed.

Closet departments and shops are not necessarily geared to the Lifestyle closet. Keep your eyes open for finds in other places:

Hardware stores have tension rods that can double your hanging space by giving you two levels instead of one. These rods can also transform an alcove into an adjunct closet. Wooden clothes-drying racks are great for airing sweaty clothes—and they fold flat for storage.

Kitchen departments are full of finds: towel racks for hanging scarves on your closet walls; stackable plastic cubes, vegetable bins, and baskets for sweaters and shirts; plastic-coated wire shelving and grid systems which give you lots of extra hanging space for shoulder bags, belts, necklaces, and chains. Wire shoe racks on wheels are more practical than shoebags.

Bath shops have wall-mounted retractable drying racks that keep your scarves and shawls visible and wrinkle free.

Stationery stores have wire "in-out" baskets ideal for stacking sweaters so they can breathe and show their colors.

Some *Closet-shop* items can be converted to other uses within your closet. Take your shoes out of the hanging shoebag and use the compartments for small-but-necessary closet accessories like sewing kit, shoe brush, shoe polish, clothes brush, etc. You might set aside one compartment for the fabric-care tags from your clothes. Or what about using your shoe caddy for stockings arranged by color? That way they'll be handy to your shoes.

Organizing *Addables* is no problem if you use your imagination:

Jewelry can be hung on decorative hooks, on pegboards, or can rest in drawers lined with Pacific silvercloth, which will keep it in place and free of tarnish.

Belts can be hung on cup hooks screwed into the bottom of a large wooden hanger. There are special pronged hangers for belts. Or you could roll them into shoebag compartments, leaving a loop of color to show for quick identification.

Hatboxes. Hats piled one on top of another work better than hatboxes. Each box takes up too much room and obscures its contents.

Small chests of drawers with see-through windows are perfect organizers for scarves, gloves, handkerchiefs, underwear, and hose. These chests are compact enough to fit into a closet.

For showcasing your wardrobe, an armoire or open shelving is your best bet. Again the principle is: What you don't see you tend to forget. There are, however, items that you may want to keep unseen—Grandma's wedding dress, a precious piece of fabric, a dress that has sentimental value but is unwearable. For these, an old trunk or suitcase, a closed garment bag, or an underbed storage unit is ideal. But unless you have an attic, don't hold onto anything just because "it might come in handy some day." Inevitably it won't. And meanwhile it uses up valuable space. The rule is: If you can't put it on your ClothesWise Chart, it has no place in your closet.

We can't all be superorganized every moment of the day. We leave for work in a rush, we come home tired, and things to be mended or dry-cleaned tend to pile up. What to do with them? The "Catch-all Chair" is your solution. Make it the one place to throw clothes that should not, for one reason or another, go back into the closet right away. It's a great safety valve for two reasons: 1) If you have somewhere to throw these clothes, you won't be tempted to hang them back in the closet. 2) If they're out in the open, they'll remind you that they need tending to.

Similarly, a small box or tray on your dresser can serve as a place to put watches, barrettes, or similar items prior to putting them away.

The "Active-Sports Tree" is a clever trick for dealing with sweaty sports gear. It can be anything from a wood valet to a brass hat rack, but the idea is to provide a decorative way of letting your gear dry out before storing it. Another idea for sportswear is to screw a line of hooks onto a closet door, one for each item: T-shirt, running pants, socks, tennis shorts, etc. Leave the door open until they're aired. This avoids piles of clothing on the floor or over chair backs.

"The Tomorrow Hook" avoids a last-minute frenzy of dressing in the morning. The night before, hang your outfit and everything you intend to wear with it on a special hook. The Tomorrow Hook can also serve to air out your clothes when you come home, before they go back behind closed doors.

Out of the closet: ome care for your Lifestyle Wardrobe

- The best way to avoid machine damage to elasticized *lingerie* is to hand wash. But not in the sink. Instead, fill a large jar with luke-warm water; add detergent. Put the garment in, screw on cap and shake it. It works faster than sudsing in the sink. If you must use a washer, put all your fragile undergarments into a nylon mesh bag before they go into the machine.

- If you can't iron a just-washed *silk or cotton shirt* right away, roll it in a damp towel, cover it with a plastic bag and put it in the refrigerator.

- A *down* garment can be machine washed. To fluff it up, put a tennis ball or clean sneaker in the dryer along with it.

- Your *pantyhose* won't wear out so fast at the heel if you rub a candle on the inside of your shoe, where it contacts your stocking.
- *Shoes* can be rid of salt stains by rubbing with a cloth or sponge dipped in a solution of 50% white vinegar and 50% water. Use an artgum eraser to remove dirt from suede shoes. Restore the shine on patent leather with a dab of petroleum jelly. Spray the rope soles of your espadrilles with silicone spray—they'll last longer.
- Keep *chains and thin necklaces* from tangling by slipping them through a drinking straw cut to size.

Taking your Lifestyle Wardrobe to the cleaners

At the Cleaners

- Before you let style seduce you, check on care factors. A high-price tag is no guarantee of a garment's life. A $500 *sequin*-covered jacket may be good for a very limited number of wearings if the sequins are gelatin; they'll dissolve in the dry-cleaning process. A dress or T-shirt with *glued-on* spangles can't be washed or dry-cleaned and will suffer the same fate.

- PLEATS can be a problem at the dry cleaner's unless you're careful to buy a part-synthetic-blend fabric. All wool, when exposed to moisture, unpleats. Stitched-down pleating is best.

- CORDUROY is subject to color loss. Stick with softer shades to minimize this.

- VELVET water-spots easily and acetate velvet especially mats down when in contact with water. Cotton and rayon velvets are more durable and better buys.

- SILK SHIRTS don't shrink but they tend to fray at stress points, so buy them large enough to allow for this.

14. The Cinderella Syndrome

For outright seductiveness there's nothing to beat evening clothes. They seem to dance right off the pages of fashion magazines and create their own fantasies without being asked. But these fantasies don't come cheap. Evening clothes are expensive and too often spend their lives in your closet, taking up space that should be allotted to a seasonless silk dress or a versatile velvet jacket. Just remember—evening clothes are like pastries in a bakery window: Look but don't give in unless you want more fat in your wardrobe than you can afford.

The Cinderella syndrome affects all of us. No matter how humdrum our lives may be we still believe that, at the eleventh hour, we'll be invited to the ball. For most of us this sort of "evening" doesn't exist.

But the stores, in their advertising and displays, work hard to convince us that our lives are a series of gala evenings out, for which they will happily provide the clothes. If we're honest with our selves, we know better. Let's recognize these fantasies for what they amount to: the Great Saturday Night Rip-Off—a dream that becomes a spending trap.

Don't let your dreams ruin your budget. Look into your newly organized closet and see what possibilities your Lifestyle Wardrobe holds. There are tricks to produce evening looks—presto-chango!— off your own rack.

There are basically two categories of dressy clothes: formal and festive.

The first rule about *formal* wear is: Don't buy unless you absolutely have to. Not even an engraved invitation to the ball warrants your dashing out to spend money on an evening gown that would delight Cinderella and dazzle the prince. After all, how many evenings of your year are likely to be spent at the palace?

There's no place in your Lifestyle Wardrobe for a formal gown unless you use it more than once a year. But for a one-time wearing there are some interesting alternatives: Try them on for size. One might be a perfect fit.

- As long as your escort is in black tie, you have more leeway than you think. A cocktail dress might do.

- Can you fake an evening look with any of the following: a caftan, loungewear, an elegant nightgown?
- Try a shiny leotard with a long skirt.
- Add sequins or gold braid to a dress you already have, if the fabric is dressy enough and you can sew.
- Borrow an evening dress from a friend.

If you can't get around the situation any other way, and you're certain you'll wear the dress at least twice this year, go ahead and buy. But:

- Buy on sale. Don't be afraid of a shopworn look. Dry cleaning and a little mending are still far cheaper than buying at regular price. And don't forget, you'll be appearing at night when flaws in clothing recede visually.

- Buy seasonless fabric. Stay away from velvet and brocade. The best choices are silk, chiffon, jersey, and beading on a lightweight material.

- You have more color freedom here than with any other items in your Lifestyle Wardrobe. An evening dress is a unique purchase that stands alone; it's not subject to the mix/match rules that govern the rest of your clothing choices.

Cinderella was lucky. Her pumpkin coach picked her up at her door. The rest of us have to worry about keeping warm on our way to the ball. A street-length coat always looks makeshift over a long skirt. An evening coat, on the other hand, is one of the least cost-efficient purchases you can make. Instead, substitute:

- A floor-length loungewear robe in velour or velvet

- A shawl or cape

- An ethnic jacket or kimono

- A rented fur

Festive dressing is less than formal and more than casual. It's everything from a patio party to a premiere. This clothing category has its rules, too: Your choice of what to wear will be guided by location, hour, and type of function. After that, you're free to bring out the fantasy. Here's where shopping in your closet for those oddities you can't bear to throw away can pay off. For instance, the thrift-shop kimono that was hand embroidered and a terrific buy. The wide woven belt from Mexico, the Lurex-threaded shawl you bought in a moment of glitter-madness.

Pull out those pieces you've never known what to do with: the peach satin camisole you discovered on sale in the lingerie department; an antique beaded handbag you bought at a bazaar. These extras can turn your daytime into nighttime clothes.

But the *basics* of your festive look come from your Lifestyle Wardrobe. In fact, special occasions are when you're going to give your Expandables a run for their money. Remember, the first rule is: Don't buy—you have it in your closet. Here's how.

ou're going to a reception or cocktail party right from work.

1. Don't change. Wear the knit dress you've worn to the office but *carry your attaché case.* When you enter the party with it, it says a lot. It explains that your busy work life doesn't allow you the time to go home and change. An attaché case always lends an air of glamour; you're on the way "up."

Solutions:

2. Wool skirt and cashmere sweater. Extras here:Tuck your hair into a Lurex beret and wear your important jewelry. Your clutch comes out of the attaché case, which can be left at the office this time, since you're more "dressed" than in the first solution.

3. If you're going on to dinner, use a basic knit dress again. This time add the following: a glittery scarf worn bandolier style, important jewelry, an evening pouch. All these items are small enough to be transported to work in your attaché case.

ou're going direct from the office to a theater opening, restaurant, or dinner at someone else's house. The occasion is dressier—no attaché-case ploy is possible here.

SITUATION:

1. The trusty knit dress again, but this time change your shoes. Slip on evening strap sandals, take along with an evening bag, and a kimono to pop over everything.

Solutions:

115

2. Remove the jacket from your suit and unbutton the blouse to reveal a satin camisole. Tuck a silk flower into the skirt waistband or pin it to the blouse.

3. Pants worn with a tank-top leotard (worn during the day beneath your shirt) wrapped with a Mexican belt. Add jewelry.

SITUATION:

ou're coming from home—or have time to go home and change before going off to a party.

Solutions:

1. Slip into pants and wear a camisole with a glittery shawl as a coverup. Add the strappy sandals, the evening bag.

2. For even more drama, wear the same pants with the tank-top leotard and fling on a feather or yarn boa.

As you've guessed by now, "Festive" is the fantasy part of dressing. Your Lifestyle Wardrobe will give you all you need to work with. Your cache of "ethnics," impulse buys, blues-chasers—even your "mistakes"—will do a comeback and spark your basics with a personal touch. They'll turn any look into yours alone. And all the "buying" was done in your own closet.

15. Real-Life Dressing

J oan's Lifestyle Chart is well balanced. Her five colors—casual-out, casual-home, work, active sports and evening—show up in almost equal blocks. "I've learned how to run my clothes life smoothly. During the course of an ordinary day I may shop for groceries, plan a dinner party, drive to my work at the Municipal Arts Society, take a quick exercise class, cook for my guests, and change into a caftan for dinner. (I only buy the ones without loose sleeves though—ever tried serving, with a yard of fabric hanging from each wrist?)

"The weekend finds us in the country and outdoors—long walks or tennis if the weather's good. I've learned to buy pretty loungewear for indoors, though. If we're reading or having dinner, why should my husband have to see me not dressed-up at home?

"My evening life is sometimes casual—in the country, mostly—but in town I want to look more formal. Most of our entertaining and going out is related to my husband's work. Similarly, the time I spend at the Society often puts me on view; whether it's raising money, giving speeches, or just program planning.

"There's one thing I feel strongly about: I dress to look great and I think of my wardrobe as a sort of deputy: it *represents* me. It has to take me through five different functions in a day. I admit to liking fairly conservative Expandables. My taupe "St. Laurent" jacket with black braid was an investment even though it *was* a copy. But look how many luncheons, speeches, cocktail parties, and even little dinners it's taken me through!

"One thing I do religiously: I inventory everything I own. If I didn't keep my closet chart up to date I'd go mad. A life like mine is dependent on good clothes planning. The red part of my Lifestyle Chart has its own organization. I prefer not to repeat an outfit for two weeks. With the purple evening blocks it's less important: Since our evening life is both city and country I can wear the same dress in both places.

"I'm a person who tends to hold onto clothes a long time. Living my kind of life has taught me that one good piece is worth a thousand costly experiments. Since my personal style doesn't change much, I've learned to go with what works, even though the price may shock me initially."

GLORIA   Gloria's Lifestyle Chart is almost all green for work. Her wardrobe looks wildly unbalanced and that's exactly why it is effective for her. "I know that now's the time for my big push in the communications world. My job at the station takes up all my time. I admit that I love the challenges.

"My day begins at 6 A.M. and sometimes runs into the wee hours. My social life is definitely impromptu: a drink after work, a late supper. Except for two or three industry galas a year, for which I've bought a few knock-out designer gowns at clearance sales, I have no need for an evening wardrobe as such.

"With my schedule, I have little time for organized sports. If I find a free hour, even if it's late, I'll do exercises or skip rope in my apartment, but that's it for the time being. 'Casual' barely exists for me and I don't have to tell you why.

"Working with a single category of dressing does simplify things. I like 'uniforms,' such as my black cashmere turtleneck and skirt, which I vary with black pants. Over these I can pop any one of a number of jackets. I consider my jackets accessories—there's nothing like them to change the look of a whole outfit instantly. I have a real repertory from scarlet velvet to banker's gray pinstripe, just like a man's.

"Obviously I put my clothes dollars where my lifestyle is. It's like betting on yourself, your talent, your career. And, in my profession, clothes are more than part of the picture—they can really give you an edge. Since I don't want to dissipate my clothing budget on things that don't help my work life at this point, I've become smart at figuring out strategies for dealing with my other activities. For example, I've got a lot of silk camisoles, all in pale evening colors, that won't show under shirts and sweaters. If I've got a late-night date, off comes my jacket and blouse, and presto—I'm ready to dance!

"What's my fashion philosophy? I figure it this way: with clothes, there's no right or wrong—there's only *effective* dressing. And I'm putting my clothes money where my goals are."

MARIKA

Marika's Lifestyle Chart reflects her varied activities: There are mostly two colors—blue and yellow for casual-out and casual-home. She works at home as a free-lance illustrator, coming into town at least once a month to meet with editors.

"There's no way I can be persuaded to give up my jeans. With two small children underfoot I need to be able to pull something on that will stand up to anything from car-pooling to sandboxes, from errands to mixing formulas. Jeans transcend the casual-in and casual-home categories on my chart. I don't have dressy clothes since our entertaining is very informal. Long skirts or evening pajamas are perfect for our frequent get-togethers at home.

"I use Addables a lot to trademark my look. They're mostly things I've collected from my single days when I traveled a lot. A giant safari bag was my best investment. I can carry my home and office in it and it's the easiest way to lend cachet to whatever I wear. A Mexican shawl thrown over a plain silk dress can look special if I'm going to meet a client, but what I love about it is that the same shawl can go over a long skirt for an evening at home.

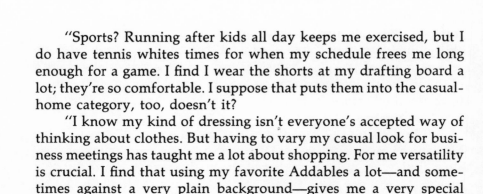

"Sports? Running after kids all day keeps me exercised, but I do have tennis whites times for when my schedule frees me long enough for a game. I find I wear the shorts at my drafting board a lot; they're so comfortable. I suppose that puts them into the casual-home category, too, doesn't it?

"I know my kind of dressing isn't everyone's accepted way of thinking about clothes. But having to vary my casual look for business meetings has taught me a lot about shopping. For me versatility is crucial. I find that using my favorite Addables a lot—and sometimes against a very plain background—gives me a very special look."

These are Lifestyle Wardrobes come to life. The women you're hearing are real people talking about their clothes. Each has a lifestyle—and a wardrobe—very different from the others. What can a corporate wife, a rising executive, and a free-lancer with small children have in common? Their wardrobes are all based squarely on *Real-life Needs.* How did they do it? They had to be their own fashion authorities. Why? Because the old fashion authorities aren't telling us how we ought to look anymore. Paris, the couture, the magazines, the designers themselves, are all saying the same thing: We'll give you the options; the rest is up to you.

Total fashion freedom is hard to deal with. But you can make it work to your advantage. How? By remembering the built-in

structure at the core of your life: the way you spend your time, what you do. Your lifestyle. And that's where today's woman, if she's smart, will look for directions now—at her own life. It doesn't come with written instructions and it's more difficult than following the trends from Milan and Paris. But once you discover it, it's a sure bet, an infallible guide. Dressing for your lifestyle will never let you down.

The Lifestyle Wardrobe: It's as simple as dressing for who you are and what you do.

REAL-LIFE DRESSING STRATEGIES: HOW THEY DO IT

SHERRY LANSING, president of 20th-Century Fox, has developed something of a uniform: pants with a silk shirt and often a blazer. "At the beginning of each season, I might buy one outfit in five or six colors."

ELLIN SALTZMAN, vice president and corporate fashion director at Saks Fifth Avenue, also advocates a uniform: a silk shirt and trousers. "In the summer I just roll up my shirt sleeves." Black is usually her main color, "Black with brights, or an occasional pale, just for shock."

NANCY REAGAN, "My wardrobe is dictated by the life I'm leading."

PHYLLIS GEORGE BROWN, wife of the governor of Kentucky, says that her style of dressing has changed with her careers. "When I was a sportscaster, I was sporty," she says. "Now I'm much more classic."

PALOMA PICASSO, jewelry designer, says her wardrobe is built around a small group of black basics. "I always have one or two pairs of black pants, several black shirts and one black dress. I wear these with bright colors. When you wear black, you can use a lot of accessories. I like big jewelry even though I'm small: little jewelry doesn't work for me. When I put a hat or a jewel on, it's the bigger the better. I can't go halfway. It has to be all or nothing."

DONNA KARAM, fashion designer, says, "Start with your neutrals on the bottom and bring in your accents on top; always have a pair of wine shoes and a wine handbag. They go with everything. Every woman must own a pair of black pants and a black skirt." Her wardrobe begins with "fabulous pants in neutral colors, like black or navy. I can dress those up or down with a sweater for day, a silk charmeuse shirt for night. I prefer to have one thing, like a sweater, in multiple colors. That's how you make a statement."

AUDREY HEPBURN, actress, says, "The rules of dressing are practically the same no matter what you spend. I want as little as possible in my closet. I want just one thing, but I want it to be right."

MARINA SCHIANO, PR consultant to Yves St. Laurent, says, "I adore exaggerated things because they go with my look. It's research, I suppose, choosing what suits you best. I'm not a normal person. I don't have a normal, standard face or size . . . so it's either exaggerate or it's a catastrophe."

LOUISE NEVELSON, sculptor, says, "Being well dressed is not a question of having expensive clothes or the 'right' clothes—but they must suit you. I like wearing lovely things . . . in the daytime, old lace dresses, Japanese robes. When I buy something new in a store I may not wear it for a year until I get used to it. My day is filled with my work and my interests. . . ."